The Royal Commission on Historical Manuscripts

Record Repositories in Great Britain

ELEVENTH EDITION

edited by Ian Mortimer

PUBLIC RECORD OFFICE

Public Record Office
Kew
Richmond
Surrey TW9 4DU

First published by HMSO 1964
Eleventh edition published
by the Public Record Office 1999

ISBN 1 873162 76 6

A catalogue card for this book
is available from the British Library

The cover illustration shows the window designed by Jane Campbell
for the City of Westminster Archives Centre, which opened in 1995.
It is reproduced by kind permission of the City Archivist.

Printed by The Cromwell Press Ltd, Trowbridge

Contents

Introduction

The purpose of *Record Repositories in Great Britain* is to collect in one manageable volume the means of contacting those institutions in Great Britain whose objectives include the systematic collection and preservation of written records other than those of their own administration and which also make regular provision for their public use.

The institutions concerned fall into four main categories:

1. National record offices and libraries financed directly by central government funds
2. Local record offices and libraries financed by local government authorities
3. Higher education libraries and departments financed mainly from central government funds through the Higher Education Funding Councils but in part by endowment and other income
4. Special libraries and archives supported by privately or charitably endowed societies and institutions.

Up to and including the ninth edition (1993) entries were arranged geographically by county. This proved to be inappropriate in the wake of local government reorganisation, and for the tenth edition (1997) a distinction was made between repositories with a national, university or special remit (part one) and those financed by local government authorities (part two). This arrangement has been preserved in the present edition.

Details are given of 319 repositories and organisations, a slight increase on the previous edition. This is only a fraction of the number of British organisations with collections of manuscript material; however it is not within the scope of this directory to list the many museums and libraries which incidentally hold manuscripts or the numerous other institutions and private owners who are prepared by arrangement to make their own records available for research. Details of repositories not found in this volume may be found on ARCHON, the archival gateway for the UK, maintained by the Commission on its website (http://www.hmc.gov.uk/). Other organisations which may be able to help students locate papers are listed in Part 5: Other Useful Addresses.

The indexes to the National Register of Archives (NRA) have now been available over the Internet (via Telnet) for four years. In addition, in 1998 a means of searching the indexes via the World Wide Web was launched. In order to help researchers use these remote methods of searching, the code for each repository on the NRA database appears in the directory after its name. Researchers may thus use the volume in conjunction with the NRA to discover more easily the major collections of each repository. Custodians may also use the NRA location number here given as a unique repository identifier for purposes such as the International Standard Archival Description, ISAD(G). Lists of collections noted on the indexes to the NRA may be consulted in the Commission's search room.

The Commission is again grateful to repositories for providing the information in this edition. I should also like to thank in particular Ian Mortimer, the editor of the volume, and Beverley Peters who checked the majority of the entries.

CJ Kitching
Secretary

Quality House, Quality Court,
Chancery Lane, London WC2A 1HP

May 1999

Notes

Telephone numbers

Some regional codes and telephone numbers (including those for London) are due to change officially on 22 April 2000. In each case where a code changes the local number will also change. When used in conjunction with the new code the new number is already effective. Dialling locally only the existing number will work until 22 April 2000, after which only the new number will work. Both old and new numbers have been given throughout this volume, the new number in parentheses.

Internet addresses

Only websites maintained by the organisation itself or its parent body (e.g. a local authority) have been included. Addresses of websites maintained by enthusiasts, whether on behalf of repositories or otherwise, have not been given. The Archives Council Wales addresses have been given for Welsh repositories lacking their own websites. Project Earl addresses (i.e. webpages of partners in the Consortium for Public Library Networking) have been included where requested by the repository.

World Wide Web addresses vary in length and complexity. Too brief or complex an address increases the chance of the required page not being found. In addition, it is difficult to give exact addresses for specific pages on some frames-based websites without losing the important context of the frame. In editing http addresses consideration has therefore been paid not only to how much information a page includes about a repository but also to the ease with which it may be found.

Opening hours and periods of closure

In addition to the regular annual periods of closure noted, virtually all repositories are closed on public holidays and for several days between Christmas and New Year.

Requirements for access

This section notes if any proof of identity or ticket is required for access to original material. Proof of identity should include a residential address. 'Letter of introduction' should be taken to mean that researchers are themselves required to write in advance or to provide an academic reference on arrival (if booking in advance is not required). Where it is necessary to obtain a reader's ticket it should be assumed that proof of identity will also be required in the first instance; some repositories will also require one or two photographs. This also applies to CARN (County Archive Research Network) readers' tickets.

Booking in advance

Certain repositories require either an appointment or a booking to be made prior to arrival at the repository. Many will not grant access otherwise, especially to microform facilities.

Fees

A few repositories levy a charge on some or all users for access to original material. Most repositories will additionally charge for copies to be made of manuscripts. Some also charge a booking fee for the use of microforms.

Wheelchair access

This indicates which repositories can accommodate wheelchair users in the search room. It does not signify other disabled facilities. Wheelchair users should always contact the repository in advance of arrival.

Research service

This indicates which repositories offer a research service in return for an hourly or half-hourly fee. Many other repositories answer limited and specific enquiries free. Some repositories can provide a list of professional research agents.

Abbreviations

The following abbreviations should be noted:

D	Designated by the bishop of a diocese as a repository for ecclesiastical records within that diocese. The name(s) of the diocese(s) and any qualifications are indicated in brackets.
HMC	Repositories recognised by the Royal Commission on Historical Manuscripts as fully meeting national standards.
M&T	Recognised by the Master of the Rolls as a repository for manorial and tithe documents under the provisions of section 144A(7) of the Law of Property Act 1922 and section 36(2) of the Tithe Act 1936, as amended by section 7(1) of the Local Government (Records) Act 1962. This recognition is being phased out in favour of HMC recognition (see above) and has not been noted where HMC recognition has been granted.
P	Appointed by the Lord Chancellor as a repository for individually specified classes of public records under the provisions of section 4 of the Public Records Act 1958.
P (Scotland)	Approved as a place of deposit for records held under the charge and superintendence of the Keeper of the Records of Scotland.

Part 1: National, University and Special Repositories in Great Britain

Aberdeen University Library, Department of Special Collections and Archives (code: 231)
DISS, Heritage Division, King's College, Aberdeen AB24 3SW

Tel 01224 272598
Fax 01224 273891
Email speclib@abdn.ac.uk
http://www.abdn.ac.uk/library/

Manager, Heritage Division:
Mr Alan Knox
Open Mon–Fri 9.30–4.30
Wheelchair access

Tel 0121 414 5838
Fax 0121 471 4691
Email special-collections@bham.ac.uk
http://www.is.bham.ac.uk/menu/index.htm

Head of Special Collections:
Miss Christine Penney
Open Mon–Fri 9–5. Closed one week in July
Letter of introduction required
Book in advance
Wheelchair access
P

BBC Written Archives Centre (code: 898)
Caversham Park, Reading RG4 8TZ

Tel 0118 946 9281/2
Fax 0118 946 1145
Email WAC.Enquiries@bbc.co.uk

The Written Archivist:
Mrs JM Kavanagh
Open Wed–Fri 9.45–1, 2–5
Letter of introduction required
Book in advance
Wheelchair access

Black Cultural Archives (code: 1443)
378 Coldharbour Lane, Brixton, London SW9 8LF

Tel 0171 738 4591
(020 7738 4591)
Fax 0171 738 7168
(020 7738 7168)
Email 106464.3650@compuserve.com

Director: Mr SH Walker
Open: Mon–Fri 10.30–4.00
Book in advance
Wheelchair access

Birmingham University Information Services, Special Collections Department (code: 150)
Main Library, University of Birmingham, Edgbaston, Birmingham B15 2TT

Bristol University Library (code: 3)
Tyndall Avenue, Bristol BS8 ITJ

Tel 0117 928 8014
Fax 0117 925 5334
Email library@bris.ac.uk
http://www.bris.ac.uk/Depts/Library/

Special Collections Librarian:
  Mr MT Richardson
Archivist: Ms Hannah Lowery
Open Mon–Fri 9.15–4.45
Letter of introduction and proof of ID
  required
Book in advance
Wheelchair access

**Bristol University Theatre
Collection (code: 811)**
Department of Drama, Cantocks
  Close, Bristol BS8 1UP

Tel 0117 928 7836
Fax 0117 928 7832
Email s.j.morris@bris.ac.uk
http://www.bris.ac.uk/Depts/Drama/
  tc.html

Keeper: Mrs Sarah Morris
Open Mon–Fri 9.15–4.45
Book in advance
No wheelchair access

British Film Institute (code: 1456)
BFI Information, 21 Stephen Street,
  London W1P 2LN

Tel 0171 255 1444
  (020 7255 1444)
Fax 0171 436 0165
  (020 7436 0165)
Email library@bfi.org.uk
http://www.bfi.org.uk/

Special Collections Manager:
  Ms Janet Moat
Open Mon, Fri 10.30–5.30; Tues,
  Thurs 10.30–8; Wed 1–8
Members ticket required
A fee may be payable
Book in advance
Wheelchair access

**British Geological Survey Library
(code: 158)**
Kingsley Dunham Centre, Keyworth,
  Nottingham NG12 5GG

Tel 0115 936 3205
Fax 0115 936 3200
Email g.mckenna@bgs.ac.uk
http://www.bgs.ac.uk/

Chief Librarian and Archivist:
  Mr Graham McKenna
Open Mon–Thurs 9–5; Fri 9–4.30
Book in advance
Wheelchair access
Research service
P

**British Library, Manuscript
Collections (code: 58)**
96 Euston Road, London NW1 2DB

Tel 0171 412 7513
  (020 7412 7513)
Fax 0171 412 7745
  (020 7412 7745)
Email mss@bl.uk
http://www.bl.uk/collections/
  manuscripts/

Director of Special Collections:
  Dr Alice Prochaska
Open Mon–Sat 9.30–5. Closed one or
  two weeks in November
Readers ticket required (letter of
  introduction in first instance)
Wheelchair access
P M&T

**British Library, Oriental and India
Office Collections (code: 59)**
96 Euston Road, London NW1 2DB

Tel 0171 412 7873
(020 7412 7873)
Fax 0171 412 7641
(020 7412 7641)
Email oioc-enquiries@bl.uk
http://www.bl.uk/collections/oriental/

Director of Special Collections:
  Dr Alice Prochaska
Open Mon–Sat 9.30–5
Readers ticket required
Wheelchair access
P

**British Medical Association Archive
(code: 1501)**
BMA House, Tavistock Square,
  London WC1H 9JP

Tel 0171 353 6588
(020 7383 6588)
Fax 0171 383 6717
(020 7383 6717)
http://www.bma.org.uk/

Archivist: Ms Emily Naish
Open Mon–Fri 9–5
Letter of introduction required
Book in advance
Wheelchair access

BT Archives (code: 1814)
Third Floor, Holborn Telephone
  Exchange, 268–270 High Holborn,
  London WC1V 7EE

Tel 0171 492 8792
(020 7492 8792)
Fax 0171 242 1967
(020 7242 1967)
Email archives@bt.com
http://www.bt.com/archives/

Group Archivist: Mr David Hay
Open Mon–Fri 10–4
Proof of ID required
Book in advance
No wheelchair access
HMC P

**Cambridge University, Centre of
South Asian Studies (code: 13)**
Laundress Lane, Cambridge CB2 1SD

Tel 01223 338094
Fax 01223 316913
Email lh222@cam.ac.uk
http://www.s-asian.cam.ac.uk/

Acting Secretary-Librarian:
  Ms Louise Houghton
Open Mon–Fri 9–1, 2–5.30. Closed in
  August
Letter of introduction required
Book in advance
No wheelchair access

**Cambridge University, Churchill
Archives Centre (code: 14)**
Churchill College, Cambridge CB3
  0DS

Tel 01223 336087
Fax 01223 336135
Email archives@chu.cam.ac.uk
http://www.chu.cam.ac.uk/archives/
  home.htm

Keeper: Dr Piers Brendon
Open Mon–Fri 9–5
Proof of ID required
Book in advance
Special arrangements for wheelchairs
HMC

**Cambridge University, King's
College Library, Modern Archive
Centre (code: 272)**
King's College, Cambridge CB2 1ST

Tel 01223 331444
Fax 01223 331891
Email jc10021@cus.cam.ac.uk
http://bear.kings.cam.ac.uk/

Archivist: Ms Jacky Cox
Open Mon–Fri 9.30–12.30, 1.30–5.15.
  Closed 6 weeks in May/June
Letter of introduction and proof of ID
  required
Book in advance
Wheelchair access

Cambridge University, Scott Polar Research Institute (code: 15)
Lensfield Road, Cambridge CB2 1ER

Tel 01223 336555
Fax 01223 336549
Email rkh10@cam.ac.uk
http://www.spri.cam.ac.uk/

Archivist: Mr Robert Headland
Open Mon–Fri 10–12.30, 2.30–5
Proof of ID required
Book in advance
Wheelchair access
P

Cambridge University, Trinity College Library (code: 16)
Trinity College, Cambridge CB1 1TQ

Tel 01223 338488
Fax 01223 338532
Email trin-lib@lists.cam.ac.uk
http://rabbit.trin.cam.ac.uk/

Librarian: Dr DJ McKitterick
Open Mon–Fri 9–5
Letter of introduction required
Book in advance
No wheelchair access

Cambridge University Library, Department of Manuscripts and University Archives (code: 12)
West Road, Cambridge CB3 9DR

Tel 01223 333000 ext 33143
  (Manuscripts), 33148 (University
  archives)
Fax 01223 333160
Email mss@ula.cam.ac.uk
http://www.lib.cam.ac.uk/MSS/

Keeper of Manuscripts and
  University Archives: Dr PNR Zutshi
Open Mon–Fri 9.30–6.45;
  S 9.30–12.45. Closed one week in
  September
Readers ticket required (letter of
  introduction in first instance)
Book in advance
Wheelchair access
P M&T D (Ely)

Royal Commonwealth Society Library
(code: 115)

Tel 01223 333198
Fax 01223 333160
Email tab@ula.cam.ac.uk
http://www.lib.cam.ac.uk/MSS/

Librarian: Miss TA Barringer

Royal Greenwich Observatory
Archives (code: 180)

Tel 01223 333056
Fax 01223 333160
Email ajp@ula.cam.ac.uk
http://www.lib.cam.ac.uk/MSS/

Archivist: Mr AJ Perkins

Canterbury Cathedral Archives (code: 54)
The Precincts, Canterbury CT1 2EH

Tel 01227 463510
Fax 01227 865222
http://www.kent.gov.uk/kcc/arts/
archives/canter.html

Cathedral Archivist: Dr Michael Stansfield
Open Mon–Thurs 9–5; first and third Sat in each month 9–1. Closed two weeks in January
Member of the CARN scheme
Book in advance
Wheelchair access
Research service
P M&T D (Canterbury: Canterbury archdeaconry)

Chethams Library (code 418)
Long Millgate, Manchester M3 1SB

Tel 0161 834 7961
Fax 0161 839 5797
Email chetlib@dial.pipex.com

Librarian: Mr Michael Powell
Open Mon–Fri 9.30–12.30, 1.30–4.30
Letter of introduction
Book in advance
Wheelchair access

Church of England Record Centre (code: 105)
15 Galleywall Road, South Bermondsey, London SE16 3PB

Tel 0171 898 1030
  (020 7898 1030)
Fax 0171 898 1031
  (020 7898 1031)
Email Chris.Pickford@c-of-e.org.uk
http://www.church-of-england.org/

Director: Mr Chris Pickford
Open Mon–Fri 10–5
Book in advance
No wheelchair access
Research service

College of Arms (code: 377)
Queen Victoria Street, London EC4V 4BT

Tel 0171 248 2762
  (020 7248 2762)
Fax 0171 248 6448
  (020 7248 6448)
http://www.kwtelecom.com/heraldry/
  collarms/

Archivist: Mr RC Yorke
Open Mon–Fri 10–4
Proof of ID required
A fee may be payable
No wheelchair access
Research service

Dr Williams's Library (code: 123)
14 Gordon Square, London WC1H 0AG

Tel 0171 387 3727
  (020 7387 3727)
Fax 0171 388 1142
  (020 7388 1142)
Email 101340.2541@compuserve.com

Director: Dr DL Wykes
Open Mon, Wed, Fri 10–5; Tues, Thurs 10–6.30. Closed first two weeks in August
No wheelchair access

Dundee University Library, Archives and Manuscripts Department (code: 254)
Tower Building, Dundee DD1 4HN

Tel 01382 344095
Fax 01382 345523
Email m.d.bolik@dundee.ac.uk
http://www.dundee.ac.uk/Archives/

University Archivist:
  Ms Patricia Whatley
Open Term Mon–Wed, Fri 9–5; Thurs
  9.30–1.30, 5–8; Sat 10–1. Vacation
  Mon–Wed, Fri 9.30–12.30; Thurs
  9.30–1.30
Readers ticket required (proof of ID
  in first instance)
Wheelchair access
Research service

**Durham University Library,
Archives and Special Collections
(code: 33)**
Palace Green Section, Palace Green,
  Durham DH1 3RN

Tel 0191 374 3001
Fax 0191 374 7481
Email PG.Library@durham.ac.uk
http://www.dur.ac.uk/Library/asc/

Sub-Librarian (Special Collections):
  Miss EM Rainey
Open Mon–Fri 9–5; Sat (term only)
  10–1
Book in advance
Wheelchair access
HMC P D (Durham)

**Edinburgh University Library,
Special Collections Department
(code: 237)**
George Square, Edinburgh EH8 9LJ

Tel 0131 650 3412
Fax 0131 650 6863
Email Special.Collections@ed.ac.uk
http://www.lib.ed.ac.uk/

Librarian, Special Collections:
  post vacant
Open Term Mon–Thurs 9–6; Fri 9–5.
  Vacation Mon–Fri 9–5. Closed
  second week in August
Readers ticket required
A fee may be payable
Book in advance
Wheelchair access

**Edinburgh University, New College
Library (code: 238)**
Mound Place, Edinburgh EH1 2UL

Tel 0131 650 8957
Fax 0131 650 6579
Email New.College.Library@ed.ac.uk
http://www.lib.ed.ac.uk/

College Librarian:
  Mrs Pamela Gilchrist
Open Term Mon–Thurs 9–9.30,
  Fri 9–5. Vacation Mon–Fri 9–5
A fee may be payable
Book in advance
Wheelchair access

**English Heritage, National
Monuments Record Centre
(code: 1585)**
Kemble Drive, Swindon, SN2 2GZ

Tel 01793 414600
Fax 01793 414606
Email info@rchme.gov.uk
http://www.english-heritage.org.uk/

Chief Executive: Ms Pam Alexander
Open Tues–Fri 9.30–5; third Sat in
  month 9.30–4
Wheelchair access
P

National Monuments Record Enquiry
and Research Services
55 Blandford Street, London W1H
3AF

Tel 0171 208 8200
(020 7208 8200)
Fax 0171 224 5333
(020 7224 5333)

Team Leader: Ms Anne Woodward
Open Tues–Fri 10–5
Wheelchair access

Exeter University Library (code: 29)
Stocker Road, Exeter EX4 4PT

Tel 01392 263870
Fax 01392 263871
Email library@exeter.ac.uk
http://www.ex.ac.uk/~ijtilsed/lib/
libintro.html

University Librarian: Mr AT Paterson
Open Mon–Fri 9–5
Readers ticket required (Letter of
introduction in first instance)
Book in advance
Wheelchair access

**Glasgow University Library, Special
Collections Department (code: 247)**
Hillhead Street, Glasgow G12 8QE

Tel 0141 330 6767
Fax 0141 330 3793
Email library@lib.gla.ac.uk
http://www.gla.ac.uk/Library/

Keeper of Special Collections: Mr
David Weston
Open Term Mon–Thurs 9–8.30,
Fri 10–5; Sat 9–12.30. Vacation
Mon–Fri 9–5; occasional
Sat 9–12.30
Readers ticket required
Wheelchair access

**Glasgow University Archives and
Business Record Centre
(code: 248)**
13 Thurso Street, Glasgow G11 6PE

Tel 0141 330 5515
Fax 0141 330 4158
Email archives@archives.gla.ac.uk
http://www.archives.gla.ac.uk/

University Archivist: Professor
Michael Moss
Open Mon–Fri 9.30–5; Thurs to 8
Readers ticket required (proof of ID
in first instance)
Book in advance
Limited wheelchair access
Research service
P (Scotland)

Scottish Brewing Archive
(code: 1127)

Tel 0141 330 6079
Fax 0141 330 4158
Email: sba@archives.gla.ac.uk
http://www.archives.gla.ac.uk/sba/

Archivist: Mrs Alma Topen
Open Tues, Thurs, Fri 9.30–5
Proof of ID required
Book in advance
No wheelchair access
Research service
P (Scotland)

**Heriot-Watt University Archives
(code: 582)**
Corporate Communications, Heriot-
Watt University, Edinburgh EH14
4AS

Tel 0131 451 3218/3219/4140
Fax 0131 451 3164
Email A.E.Jones@hw.ac.uk
http://www.hw.ac.uk/archive/

University Archivist: Ms Ann Jones
Open Mon–Fri 9.30–4.45
Book in advance
Wheelchair access

**House of Lords Record Office
(code: 61)**
House of Lords, London SW1A 0PW

Tel 0171 219 3074
(020 7219 3074)
Fax 0171 219 2570
(020 7219 2570)
Email hlro@parliament.uk
http://www.parliament.uk/

Clerk of the Records:
Mr Steve Ellison
Open Mon–Fri 9.30–5. Tues to 8
when the House is sitting (one
week's notice required). Closed
two weeks in November
Readers should show confirmation of
appointment and ID at Pass Office
Wheelchair access

**Hull University, Brynmor Jones
Library (code: 50)**
Cottingham Road, Hull HU6 7RX

Tel 01482 465265
Fax 01482 466205
Email archives@acs.hull.ac.uk
http://www.hull.ac.uk/lib/archives/

University Archivist:
Mr Brian Dyson
Open Mon–Fri 9–1 2–5. Mon to 9
by appointment.
Proof of ID required
Book in advance
Wheelchair access
M&T

**Imperial War Museum, Department
of Documents (code: 62)**
Lambeth Road, London SE1 6HZ

Tel 0171 416 5221/2/3
(020 7416 5221/2/3)
Fax 0171 416 5374
(020 7416 5374)
Email docs@iwm.org.uk
http://www.iwm.org.uk/

Keeper of the Department of
Documents: Mr RWA Suddaby
Open Mon–Sat 10–5. Closed last two
full weeks in November
Book in advance
Special arrangements for wheelchairs
P

**Institution of Civil Engineers
(code: 107)**
1–7 Great George Street, London
SW1P 3AA

Tel 0171 222 7722 ext 2043
(020 7222 7722 ext 2043)
Fax 0171 976 7610
(020 7976 7610)
Email archive@ice.org.uk
http://www.ice.org.uk/

Librarian: Mr Michael Chrimes
Open Mon–Fri 9.15–5.30
Letter of introduction required
Book in advance
Wheelchair access
Research service

**Institution of Electrical Engineers
(code: 108)**
Archives Department, Savoy Place,
London WC2R 0BL

Tel 0171 344 8436
(020 7344 8436)
Fax 0171 344 5395
(020 7344 5395)
Email archives@iee.org.uk
http://www.iee.org.uk/Archives/
archives.htm

Archivist: Mrs Lenore Symons
Open Mon 10.30–5; Tues–Fri 10–5
Proof of ID required
Book in advance
Special arrangements for wheelchairs

**Institution of Mechanical Engineers,
Information and Library Service
(code: 381)**
1 Birdcage Walk, London SW1H 9JJ

Tel 0171 973 1265
(020 7973 1265)
Fax 0171 222 8762
(020 7222 8762)
Email k_moore@imeche.org.uk
http://www.imeche.org.uk/ils/
archive.htm

Senior Librarian and Archivist:
  Mr Keith Moore
Open Mon–Fri 9.15–5.30
Book in advance
Special arrangements for wheelchairs
Research service

**Ironbridge Gorge Museum Library
and Archives (code: 491)**
The Wharfage, Ironbridge, Telford
  TF8 7AW

Tel 01952 432141
Fax 01952 432237
Email igmt@vtel.co.uk
http://www.vtel.co.uk/igmt/

Librarian: Mr John Powell
Documentation Supervisor:
  Ms J Smith
Open Mon–Fri 9–5.30
Book in advance
No wheelchair access

Keele University Library (code: 172)
Keele ST5 5BG

Tel 01782 583237
Fax 01782 711553
Email lia27@keele.ac.uk
http://www.keele.ac.uk/depts/li/
  libinf.htm

Special Collections and Archives
  Assistant: Miss Helen Burton
Open Mon–Fri 9–5. Closed five days
  at Easter, ten days in the summer
Readers ticket required for
  Wedgwood & Spode MSS. Proof of
  ID required for other collections
Book in advance
Wheelchair access

Lambeth Palace Library (code: 109)
London SE1 7JU

Tel 0171 898 1400
(020 7898 1400)
Fax 0171 928 7932
(020 7928 7932)

Librarian: Dr Richard Palmer
Open Mon–Fri 10–5. Closed for ten
  days from Good Friday
Letter of introduction and proof of ID
  required
Special arrangements for wheelchairs
P M&T

Leeds University, Brotherton Library, Department of Special Collections (code: 206)
Leeds, LS2 9JT

Tel 0113 233 5518
Fax 0113 233 5561
Email special-collections
   @library.leeds.ac.uk
http://www.leeds.ac.uk/library/spcoll/

University Librarian and Keeper of
   the Brotherton Collection:
   Mrs LJ Brindley
Head of Special Collections:
   Mr CDW Sheppard
Open Mon–Thurs 9–7; Fri 9.30–7;
Sat 10–1. Summer holiday
Mon–Thurs 9–5; Fri 9.30–5;
Sat 10–1. Closed Sat in late July
and August
Letter of introduction required
Wheelchair access

Brotherton Collection (code: 1471)

Tel 0113 233 5518
Fax 0113 233 5561
Email special-
   collections@library.leeds.ac.uk
http://www.leeds.ac.uk/library/spcoll/

Head of Special Collections:
   Mr CDW Sheppard

Liddle Collection (code: 1455)

Tel 0113 233 5566
Fax 0113 233 5561
Email p.h.liddle@leeds.ac.uk
http://www.leeds.ac.uk/library/spcoll/
   liddle/

Keeper: Dr PH Liddle
Open by arrangement
Letter of introduction required
Wheelchair access

Linnean Society of London (code: 110)
Burlington House, Piccadilly, London
   W1V 0LQ

Tel 0171 434 4479/4470
   (020 7434 4479/4470)
Fax 0171 287 9364
   (020 7287 9364)
Email Gina@linnean.demon.co.uk
http://www.linnean.org.uk/

Librarian and Archivist:
   Miss Gina Douglas
Open Mon–Fri 10–5
Proof of ID required
Book in advance
No wheelchair access

Liverpool University, Department of Special Collections and Archives (code: 141)
PO Box 123, Liverpool L69 3DA

Tel 0151 794 2696
Fax 0151 794 2681
Email archives@liv.ac.uk
http://sca.lib.liv.ac.uk/collections/
   index.html

Head of Special Collections and
   Archives: Dr Maureen Watry
Archivist: Mr Adrian Allen
Open Mon–Fri 9.30–4.45
Proof of ID required
Book in advance
Wheelchair access

London Guildhall University, Fawcett Library (code: 106)
Calcutta House, Old Castle Street, London E1 7NT

Tel 0171 320 1189
  (020 7320 1189)
Fax 0171 320 1188
  (020 7320 1188)
Email fawcett@lgu.ac.uk
http://www.lgu.ac.uk/fawcett/
  main.htm

Archivist: Ms Anna Greening
Open Term Mon 10.15–8.30;
  Wed 9–8.30; Thurs–Fri 9–5.
  Vacation Mon, Wed–Fri 9–5
Library membership required
  (proof of ID in first instance)
A fee may be payable
Special arrangements for wheelchairs

London University, Imperial College Archives (code: 98)
Room 455, Sherfield Building, Imperial College, London SW7 2AZ

Tel 0171 594 8850
  (020 7594 8850)
Fax 0171 584 3763
  (020 7584 3763)
Email a.barrett@ic.ac.uk
http://www.lib.ic.ac.uk/

College Archivist: Ms Anne Barrett
Open Mon–Fri 10–12.30, 2–5
Letter of introduction required
Book in advance
Special arrangements for wheelchairs

London University: Institute of Advanced Legal Studies (code: 1697)
Charles Clore House, 17 Russell Square, London WC1B 5DR

Tel 0171 637 1731
  (020 7637 1731)
Fax 0171 436 8224
  (020 7436 8824)
Email ials.lib@sas.ac.uk
http://ials.sas.ac.uk/
Librarian: Mr Jules Winterton
Archivist: Ms Clare Cowling
Open: Mon–Fri 9.30–8; Sat 10–5.30.
  Closed last two weeks in September
Proof of ID required
Book in advance
Wheelchair access

London University, Institute of Commonwealth Studies (code: 101)
27–28 Russell Square, London WC1B 5DS

Tel 0171 862 8844
  (020 7862 8844)
Fax 0171 862 8820
  (020 7862 8820)
Email icommlib@sas.ac.uk
http://www.ihr.sas.ac.uk/ics/
  archives.html

Archivist: Mr David Ward
Open Term Mon–Fri 9.30–6.30.
  Vacation Mon–Fri 9.30–5.30
Proof of ID and letter of
  introduction required
A fee may be payable
No wheelchair access

London University, Institute of Education (code: 366)
20 Bedford Way, London WC1H 0AL

Tel 0171 612 6093
  (020 7612 6063)
Fax 0171 612 6093
  (020 7612 6093)
Email j.haynes@ioe.ac.uk
http://www.ioe.ac.uk/library/

Archivist: Ms Jennifer Haynes
Open 9.30–12.30; 1.30–5
Proof of ID required
Book in advance
Wheelchair access

London University, King's College Archives (code: 100)
Strand, London WC2R 2LS

Tel 0171 848 2015/2187
(020 7848 2015/2187)
Fax 0171 848 2760
(020 7848 2760)
Email archives.web@kcl.ac.uk
http://www.kcl.ac.uk/kis/archives/
newhome.htm

Director of Archive Services:
 Miss Patricia Methven
Open Term Mon–Fri 9.30–5.30.
 July–August Mon–Fri 9.30–4.30.
 Closed last two weeks in August
Proof of ID required
Book in advance
Wheelchair access
P

Liddell Hart Centre for Military
 Archives (code: 99)

Tel 0171 848 2015/2187
(020 7848 2015/2187)
Fax 0171 848 2760
(020 7848 2760)
Email archives.web@kcl.ac.uk
http://www.kcl.ac.uk/lhcma/top.htm

Director of Archive Services:
 Miss Patricia Methven
Letter of introduction required

London University, London School of Economics, British Library of Political and Economic Science (code: 97)
10 Portugal Street, London WC2A 2HD

Tel 0171 955 7223
(020 7955 7223)
Fax 0171 955 7454
(020 7955 7454)
Email Document@lse.ac.uk
http://www.lse.ac.uk/blpes/archives/

Archivist: Miss SK Donnelly
Open Term & Easter vacation
 Mon–Thurs 10–7.30; Fri 10–5.30;
 Sat 11–5.30. Christmas & Summer
 vacation Mon–Thurs 10–7.30; Fri
 10–5. Closed for one week at Easter
Readers ticket required (proof of ID
 in first instance)
Book in advance
Wheelchair access

London University, School of Oriental and African Studies Library (code: 102)
Thornhaugh Street, Russell Square,
 London WC1H 0XG

Tel 0171 323 6112
(020 7323 6112)
Fax 0171 636 2834
(020 7636 2834)
Email docenquiry@soas.ac.uk
http://www.soas.ac.uk/library/

Archivist: Mrs Rosemary Seton
Open Mon–Thurs 9–7; Fri 9–5.
 Summer vacation Mon–Fri 9–5.
 Occasional Sat by arrangement.
 Closed for a week in June
Readers ticket required (letter of
 introduction in first instance)
Book in advance
Wheelchair access

London University, University College London, Manuscripts Room (code: 103)
Library Services, Gower Street, London WC1E 6BT

Tel 0171 387 7050 ext 7796
(020 7387 7050 ext 7796)
Fax 0171 380 7727
(020 7380 7727)
Email mssrb@ucl.ac.uk
http://www.ucl.ac.uk/Library/special-coll/

Archivist: Ms Gillian Furlong
Open Term Mon, Thurs, Fri 10–5; Tues, Wed 10–7. Vacation Mon–Fri 10–5. Closed one week at Easter
Readers ticket required (letter of introduction in first instance)
Book in advance
A fee may be payable
Wheelchair access

University of London Library (code: 96)
Palaeography Room, Senate House, Malet Street, London WC1E 7HU

Tel 0171 862 8475
(020 7862 8475)
Fax 0171 862 8480
(020 7862 8480)
Email rvyse@ull.ac.uk
http://www.ull.ac.uk/ull/

Archivist: Miss RF Vyse
Open Mon 9.30–8.45; Tues–Fri 9.30–6; Sat 9.30–1, 2–5.15
Readers ticket required
Book in advance (a fee may be payable otherwise)
Wheelchair access
M&T

Manchester University, John Rylands University Library of Manchester (code: 133)
150 Deansgate, Manchester M3 3EH

Tel 0161 834 5343
Fax 0161 834 5574
Email j.r.hodgson@man.ac.uk
http://rylibweb.man.ac.uk/

Head of Special Collections: Dr Peter McNiven
Open Mon–Fri 10–5.30; Sat 10–1
Readers ticket required (letter of introduction in first instance)
Book in advance
No wheelchair access
M&T

Methodist Archives and Research Centre (code: 135)

Tel 0161 834 5343
Fax 0161 834 5574
Email pnockles@fs1.li.man.ac.uk
http://rylibweb.man.ac.uk/data1/dg/text/method.html

Librarian in charge: Dr Peter Nockles
Archivist: Mr Gareth Lloyd

Museum of London Library (code: 389)
150 London Wall, London EC2Y 5HN

Tel 0171 814 5588
(020 7814 5588)
Fax 0171 600 1058
(020 7600 1058)
http://www.museumoflondon.org.uk/

Library Officer: Ms Sally Brooks
Open Mon–Fri 10–5
Letter of introduction required
Book in advance
Wheelchair access
P

Museum of Welsh Life (code: 1068)
St Fagan's, Cardiff CF5 6XB

Tel 01222 573500 ext 437
 (029 2057 3500 ext 437)
Fax 01222 573490
 (029 2057 3490)

Archivist: Mr Arwyn Lloyd Hughes
Open Mon–Fri 9.30–1, 1.45–4.30
Book in advance
Wheelchair access

**National Archives of Scotland
(code: 234)**
HM General Register House,
 Edinburgh EH1 3YY

Tel 0131 535 1314
Fax 0131 557 9569
Email research@nas.gov.uk

Keeper of Records of Scotland:
 Mr PM Cadell
Open Mon–Fri 9–4.45. HM General
 Register House closed first two
 weeks and West Register House
 third week in November
Readers ticket required (proof of ID
 in first instance)
Wheelchair access
P (Scotland)

N.B. Maintains the National Register
 of Archives (Scotland)

**National Army Museum, Department
of Archives, Photographs, Film and
Sound (code: 63)**
Royal Hospital Road, Chelsea,
 London SW3 4HT

Tel 0171 730 0717 ext 2214/2
 (020 7730 0717 ext 2214/2)
Fax 0171 823 6573
 (020 7823 6573)
Email info@national-army-museum.
 ac.uk
http://www.national-army-museum.
 ac.uk/

Head of Department of Archives:
 Dr Peter Boyden
Open Tues–Sat 10–4.30. Closed last
 two full weeks in October
Readers ticket required (letter of
 introduction in first instance)
Wheelchair access
P

**National Gallery Library and
Archive (code: 345)**
Trafalgar Square, London WC2N
 5DN

Tel 0171 839 3321
 (020 7839 3321)
Fax 0171 753 8179
 (020 7753 8179)
Email david.carter@ng-london.org.uk
http://www.nationalgallery.org.uk/

Archivist : Mr David Carter
Open by appointment
Book in advance (proof of ID in first
 instance)
Wheelchair access
P

**National Library of Scotland,
Department of Manuscripts
(code: 233)**
George IV Bridge, Edinburgh EH1
 1EW

Tel 0131 226 4531/0131 459 4531
  ext 2119
Fax 0131 220 6662
Email mss@nls.uk
http://www.nls.uk/

Director of Special Collections:
  Dr Murray Simpson
Open Mon, Tues, Thurs,
  Fri 9.30–8.30; Wed 10–8.30; Sat
  9.30–1. Closed first week in October
Readers ticket required
Wheelchair access

**National Library of Wales,
Department of Manuscripts and
Records (code: 210)**
Aberystwyth SY23 3BU

Tel 01970 632800
Fax 01970 632883
Email ymh.lc@llgc.org.uk
http://www.llgc.org.uk/

Keeper of Manuscripts and Records:
  Mr Gwyn Jenkins
Open Mon–Fri 9.30–6; Sat 9.30–5.
  Closed first full week in October
Readers ticket required
Wheelchair access
Research service
P M&T D (Province of Wales)

**National Maritime Museum,
Manuscripts Section (code: 64)**
Greenwich, London SE10 9NF

Tel 0181 312 6691
  (020 8312 6691)
Fax 0181 312 6722
  (020 8312 6722)
Email manuscripts@nmm.ac.uk
http://www.nmm.ac.uk/

Manuscript Subject Specialist:
  Mr Clive Powell
Open Mon–Fri 10–4.45. Sat by
  appointment. Closed one week in
  February
Book in advance
Readers ticket required
Wheelchair access
P

**National Museum of Labour History
(code: 394)**
103 Princess Street, Manchester M1
6DD

Tel 0161 228 7212
Fax 0161 237 5965

Director: Dr N Mansfield
Archivist/Librarian: Mr Stephen Bird
Open Mon–Fri 10–5
Book in advance
Special arrangements for wheelchairs

**National Museums and Galleries on
Merseyside, Maritime Archives and
Library (code: 136)**
Merseyside Maritime Museum,
  Albert Dock, Liverpool L3 4AQ

Tel 0151 207 0001 ext 4418
Fax 0151 478 4590
Email
  maritime@nmgmnh1.demon.co.uk
http://www.nmgm.org.uk/

Keeper of Maritime Museum:
  Mr Mike Stammers
Open Tues–Thurs 10.30–4.30
Readers ticket required
Book in advance
A fee may be payable
Wheelchair access
Research service
P

National Portrait Gallery Archive (code: 1082)
Heinz Archive and Library, St
  Martin's Place, London WC2H 0HE
  (entrance in Orange Street)

Tel 0171 306 0055
  (020 7306 0055)
Fax 0171 306 0056
  (020 7306 0056)
http://www.npg.org.uk/archive.htm

Head of Archives and Library:
  Mr Robin Francis
Open Mon–Fri 10–5
Proof of ID required
Book in advance
Wheelchair access
P

Natural History Museum (code: 60)
Cromwell Road, London SW7 5BD

Tel 0171 938 9238
  (020 7938 9238)
Fax 0171 938 9290
  (020 7938 9290)
http://www.nhm.ac.uk/

Archivist and Records Officer:
  post vacant
Open Mon–Fri 10–4
Readers ticket required
Book in advance
Wheelchair access
P

Newcastle upon Tyne University, Robinson Library (code: 186)
Newcastle upon Tyne NE2 4HQ

Tel 0191 222 7671
Fax 0191 222 6235
Email lesley.gordon@ncl.ac.uk
http://www.ncl.ac.uk/library/speccoll/
  spechome.html

Special Collections Librarian:
  Dr Lesley Gordon
Open Mon–Fri 9.15–5
Proof of ID and letter of introduction
  required
Book in advance
Wheelchair access

Nottingham University, Department of Manuscripts and Special Collections (code: 159)
Hallward Library, University Park,
  Nottingham NG7 2RD

Tel 0115 951 4565
Fax 0115 951 4558
Email mss-library@nottingham.ac.uk
http://mss.library.nottingham.ac.uk/

Keeper of the Manuscripts:
  Dr Dorothy Johnston
Open Mon–Fri 9–1, 1.30–5. Closed
  one week in September
Readers ticket required (proof of ID
  in first instance)
Book in advance
Wheelchair access
P M&T

Oxford University, Bodleian Library, Department of Special Collections and Western Manuscripts (code: 161)
Broad Street, Oxford OX1 3BG

Tel 01865 277158
Fax 01865 277187
Email
  western.manuscripts@bodley.ox.ac.uk
http://www.bodley.ox.ac.uk/guides/
  wmss/

Keeper of Special Collections and
  Western Manuscripts:
  Mrs Mary Clapinson
Open Term Mon–Fri 9–10; Sat 9–1.
  Vacation Mon–Fri 9–7; Sat 9–1.
Readers ticket required (letter of
  introduction in first instance)
A fee may be payable
Wheelchair access
M&T

**Oxford University, Bodleian Library,
Rhodes House Library (code: 162)**
South Parks Road, Oxford OX1 3RG

Tel 01865 270909
Fax 01865 270912
Email rhodes.house.library
  @bodley.ox.ac.uk
http://www.bodley.ox.ac.uk/boris/
  guides/rhl/rhl01.html

Librarian: Mr John Pinfold
Open Term Mon–Fri 9–7. Vacation
  Mon–Fri 9–5. Sat 9–1 all year.
  Closed week following August
  bank holiday
Readers ticket required (letter of
  introduction in first instance)
A fee may be payable
Special arrangements for wheelchairs

**Oxford University, Nuffield College
Library (code: 163)**
Oxford OX1 1NF

Tel 01865 278550
Fax 01865 278621
Email eleanor.vallis@nuf.ox.ac.uk
http://www.nuff.ox.ac.uk/library/

Librarian: Mr James Legg
Open Mon–Fri 9.30–5.30; Sat 9.30–1
  (not in summer holiday). Closed in
  August
Letter of introduction required
Book in advance
Wheelchair access

**Oxford University, Regent's Park
College, Angus Library (code: 469)**
Pusey Street, Oxford OX1 2LB

Tel 01865 288142
Fax 01865 288121
Email sue.mills@regents.ox.ac.uk
http://www.rpc.ox.ac.uk/

Librarian/Archivist: Mrs Susan Mills
Open Mon–Fri 9.30–4. Closed for two
  weeks at Easter and most of August
Letter of introduction required
Book in advance
A fee may be payable
No wheelchair access

**Oxford University, St Antony's
College, Middle East Centre
(code: 165)**
Oxford OX2 6JF

Tel 01865 284706
Fax 01865 311475
Email clare.brown@sant.ox.ac.uk
http://www.sant.ox.ac.uk/

Fellow in Charge: Dr D Hopwood
Archivist: Mrs Clare Brown
Open Mon–Fri 9.30–12.45; 1.45–5.15.
  Closed for one week at Easter and
  four weeks in summer
Letter of introduction required
Book in advance
A fee may be payable
Special arrangements for wheelchairs

Post Office Archives and Record Centre (code: 813)
Freeling House, Phoenix Place,
  Mount Pleasant Complex, London
  EC1A 1BB

Tel 0171 239 2570
  (020 7239 2570)
Fax 0171 239 2576
  (020 7239 2576)
Email mick.bowden@postoffice.co.uk

Archives Manager: Mr Martin Rush
Open Mon–Fri 9–4.15
Proof of ID required
Wheelchair access
P

Public Record Office (code: 66)
Ruskin Avenue, Kew, Richmond
  TW9 4DU

Tel 0181 876 3444
  (020 8876 3444)
Fax 0181 878 8905
  (020 8878 8905)
Email enquiry@pro.gov.uk
http://www.pro.gov.uk/

Keeper of Public Records:
  Mrs Sarah Tyacke
Open Mon–Sat 9.30–5. Closed first
  two weeks in December
Readers ticket required (proof of ID
  in first instance)
Wheelchair access
P M&T

Pusey House Library (code: 164)
Pusey House, 61 St Giles, Oxford
  OX1 3LZ

Tel 01865 278415
Fax 01865 278415
http://web.ukonline.co.uk/pusey.
  house/

Archivist and Chaplain:
  Revd Dr Peter Groves
Open Mon–Fri 9.15–12.45, 2–4.45.
  Closed during August
Readers ticket required (letter of
  introduction in first instance)
Book in advance
Special arrangements for wheelchairs

Reading University Library (code: 6)
PO Box 223, Whiteknights, Reading
  RG6 6AE

Tel 0118 931 8776
Fax 0118 931 6636
Email g.m.c.bott@reading.ac.uk
http://www.rdg.ac.uk/SerDepts/vl/

Keeper of Archives and
  Manuscripts: Mr Michael Bott
Open Mon–Fri 9–5. Closed in
  August
Book in advance
Wheelchair access

Reading University, Rural History Centre (code: 7)
PO Box 229, Whiteknights, Reading
  RG6 6AG

Tel 0118 931 8666
Fax 0118 975 1264
Email J.H.Brown@reading.ac.uk
http://www.rdg.ac.uk/Instits/ims/

Archivist: Dr JH Brown
Open Mon–Thurs 9.30–1, 2–5;
  Fri 9.30–1, 2–4.30
Book in advance
Wheelchair access
Research service

Religious Society of Friends (Quakers) Library (code: 111)
Friends House, 173–177 Euston
  Road, London NW1 2BJ

Tel 0171 663 1135
(020 7663 1135)
Fax 0171 663 1001
(020 7663 1001)
Email library@quaker.org.uk
http://www.quaker.org.uk/

Librarian: Mr Malcolm Thomas
Open: Mon, Tues, Thurs, Fri 1–5;
  Wed 10–5
Letter of introduction required
Book in advance for microform
  facilities
A fee may be payable for access to
  Digest Registers (on microform) of
  births, marriages and burials
Wheelchair access

Royal Air Force Museum,
Department of Research and
Information Services (code: 67)
Grahame Park Way, Hendon, London
  NW9 5LL

Tel 0181 205 2266 ext 273
  (020 8205 2266 ext 273)
Fax 0181 200 1751
  (020 8200 1751)
Email rafmus@dircon.co.uk
http://www.rafmuseum.org.uk/

Keeper of Research and Information
  Services: Mr PJV Elliott
Open Mon–Fri 10–5
Book in advance
Special arrangements for wheelchairs
P

Royal Botanic Garden Edinburgh
(code: 235)
The Library, 20a Inverleith Row,
  Edinburgh EH3 5LR

Tel 0131 552 7171
Fax 0131 248 2901
Email library@rbge.org.uk
http://www.rbge.org.uk/

Chief Librarian: Mrs Jane Hutcheon
Open Mon–Thurs 9.30–4.30;
  Fri 9.30–4
Letter of introduction required
Book in advance
Wheelchair access

Royal Botanic Gardens, Kew
(code: 68)
Library and Archives, Kew,
  Richmond, Surrey TW9 3AB

Tel 0181 332 5411/5417
  (020 8332 5411/5417)
Fax 0181 322 5430
  (020 8332 5430)
Email library@rbgkew.org.uk
http://www.rbgkew.org.uk/

Acting Head of Library and
  Archives: Mr John Flanagan
Open Mon–Fri 9–5
Readers ticket required
Book in advance
Wheelchair access
P

Royal College of Obstetricians and
Gynaecologists (code: 1538)
College Archives, 27 Sussex Place,
  Regents Park, London NW1 4RG

Tel 0171 772 6277
  (020 7772 6277)
Fax 0171 723 0575
  (020 7723 0575)
Email archives@rcog.org.uk
http://www.rcog.org.uk/

Archivist: Ms Clare Cowling
Open: Tues, Fri 9.30–5.30;
  Wed 10.30–2
Book in advance
Wheelchair access

Royal College of Physicians and Surgeons of Glasgow (code: 250)
234–242 St Vincent Street, Glasgow
 G2 5RJ

Tel 0141 221 6072
Fax 0141 221 1804
Email james.beaton@rcpsglasg.ac.uk
http://www.rcpsglasg.ac.uk/
 library.html

Archivist/Librarian: Mr James Beaton
Open Mon–Fri 9.15–5.00
Book in advance
No wheelchair access

Royal College of Physicians of London (code: 113)
11 St Andrews Place, Regents Park,
 London NW1 4LE

Tel 0171 935 1174 ext 312/3
 (020 7935 1174 ext 312/3)
Fax 0171 486 3729
 (020 7486 3729)
Email: info@rcplondon.ac.uk

Archivist and Records Manager:
 post vacant
Open Mon–Fri 9–5
Book in advance
Wheelchair access
P

Royal College of Surgeons of England (code: 114)
35–43 Lincoln's Inn Fields, London
 WC2A 3PN

Tel 0171 405 3474 ext 3008
 (020 7405 3474 ext 3008)
Fax 0171 405 4438
 (020 7405 4438)
Email library@rcseng.ac.uk
http://www.rcseng.ac.uk/

Archivist: Claire Jackson
Open Mon–Fri 9–6. Closed in
 August
Letter of introduction required
Book in advance
No wheelchair access
P

Royal Commission on the Ancient and Historical Monuments of Scotland: National Monuments Record of Scotland (code: 551)
John Sinclair House, 16 Bernard
 Terrace, Edinburgh EH8 9NX

Tel 0131 662 1456
Fax 0131 662 1477/1499
Email nmrs@rcahms.gov.uk
http://www.rcahms.gov.uk/

Secretary: Mr RJ Mercer
Open Mon–Thurs 9.30–4; Fri 9.30–4
Wheelchair access
P (Scotland)

Royal Commission on the Ancient and Historic Monuments of Wales: National Monuments Record of Wales (code: 1952)
Crown Building, Plas Crug,
 Aberystwyth SY23 1NJ

Tel 01970 621233
Fax 01970 627701
Email nmr.wales@rcahmw.org.uk
http://www.rcahmw.org.uk/

Head of Library and Archive:
 Mrs Hilary Malaws
Open: Mon–Fri 9.30–4.00; restricted
 service 1.00–2.00
Letter of intorduction
Book in advance
Wheelchair access
P

**Royal Geographical Society
(code: 402)**
1 Kensington Gore, London SW7
2AR

Tel 0171 591 3000
(020 7591 3000)
Fax 0171 591 3001
(020 7591 3001)
Email info@rgs.org
http://www.rgs.org/

Keeper: Dr Andrew Tatham
Archives Assistant: Mr Huw Thomas
Open Fri 11–5. Closed four weeks in
  summer
Letter of introduction required
Book in advance
Wheelchair access

**Royal Institute of British
Architects' Library (code: 104)**
Manuscripts and Archives
  Collection, 66 Portland Place,
  London W1N 4AD

Tel 0171 307 3615
(020 7307 3615)
Fax 0171 631 1802
(020 7631 1802)
Email jane.collings@inst.riba.org
http://www.riba.org/

Archivist: Ms Jane Collings
Open Mon 1.30–5; Tues 10–8;
  Wed–Fri 10–5. Closed in August
A fee may be payable
Wheelchair access
Research service

British Architectural Library,
Drawings Collection
21 Portman Square, London W1H
  9HF

Tel 0171 580 5533 ext 4801
(020 7580 5533 ext 4801)
Fax 0171 486 3797
(020 7486 3797)

Curator of Drawings: Mr Charles
  Hind
Open Tues–Thurs 10–1, 2–5.
  Closed in August
Book in advance
A fee may be payable
Wheelchair access

**Royal Institution of Great Britain
(code: 116)**
21 Albemarle Street, London W1X
  4BS

Tel 0171 409 2992
(020 7409 2992)
Fax 0171 629 3569
(020 7629 3569)
Email ril@ri.ac.uk
http://www.ri.ac.uk/Library/

Director of Collections: Dr FAJL
  James
Open Mon–Fri 10–5.30
Letter of introduction required
Book in advance
Wheelchair access

Royal Naval Museum (code: 1070)
HM Naval Base (PP66), Portsmouth
PO1 3NU

Tel 01705 727562
(023 9272 7562)
Fax 01705 727575
(023 9272 7575)

Curator of Manuscripts:
  Mr Matthew Sheldon
Open Mon–Fri 10–5
Book in advance
Wheelchair access

Royal Society (code: 117)
6 Carlton House Terrace, London
SW1Y 5AG

Tel 0171 451 2606
(020 7451 2606)
Fax 0171 930 2170
(020 7930 2170)
Email library@royalsoc.ac.uk
http://www.royalsoc.ac.uk/

Head of Fellowship and Information
Services: Ms Mary Nixon
Archivist: Ms Joanne Corden
Open Mon–Fri 10–5
Proof of ID required
Book in advance
Wheelchair access

**St Andrews University Library
(code: 227)**
North Street, St Andrews KY16 9TR

Tel 01334 462324
Fax 01334 462282
Email nhr1@st-and.ac.uk
http://www-library.st-and.ac.uk/
main.html

Keeper of Manuscripts and
Muniments: Dr Norman Reid
Open Term Mon–Wed, Fri 9–5; Thurs
9–9; Sat 9–12.15. Vacation 9–5
Readers ticket required
Wheelchair access
P (Scotland)

Science Museum Library (code: 69)
Imperial College Road, South
Kensington, London SW7 5NH

Tel 0171 938 8234/8218
(020 7938 8234/8218)
Fax 0171 938 9714
(020 7938 9714)
Email smlinfo@nmsi.ac.uk
http://www.nmsi.ac.uk/library/

Archivist: Mr Robert Sharp
Open Mon–Sat 9.30–5
Readers ticket required (proof of ID
in first instance)
Wheelchair access
P

**Science Museum, National Railway
Museum Reading Room (code: 756)**
Leeman Road, York YO26 4XJ

Tel 01904 621261
Fax 01904 611112
Email nrm.library@nmsi.ac.uk
http://www.nmsi.ac.uk/nrm/

Head of Library & Archive
Collections Division:
Mr DW Hopkin
Curator, Archive Collections: Mr R
Taylor
Open Mon–Sun 10–6
Readers ticket required
Book in advance
Wheelchair access

**Scottish Catholic Archives
(code: 240)**
Columba House, 16 Drummond Place,
Edinburgh EH3 6PL

Tel 0131 556 3661

Keeper: Dr Christine Johnson
Open Mon–Fri 9.30–1, 2–4.30
Letter of introduction required
Book in advance
No wheelchair access

**Sheffield University Library, Special
Collections and Library Archives
Department (code: 200)**
Western Bank, Sheffield S10 2TN

Tel 0114 222 7230
Fax 0114 222 7290
Email l.aspden@sheffield.ac.uk
http://www.shef.ac.uk/~lib/special/
  special.html

Curator of Special Collections and
  Archivist: Mr Lawrence Aspden
Open Mon–Fri 9.30–1, 2–4.30
Readers ticket required (letter of
  introduction in first instance)
Book in advance
Wheelchair access

**Society of Antiquaries of London
(code: 118)**
Burlington House, Piccadilly, London
W1V 0HS

Tel 0171 734 0193/0171 437 9954
  (020 7734 0193/020 7437 9954)
Fax 0171 287 6967
  (020 7287 6967)
Email library@sal.org.uk

Librarian: Mr EB Nurse
Open Mon–Fri 10–5. Closed in
  August
Letter of introduction required
Book in advance
Wheelchair access

**Southampton University Library
(code: 738)**
Highfield, Southampton SO17 1BJ

Tel 01703 593724/592721
  (023 8059 3724/2721)
Fax 01703 593007
  (023 8059 3007)
Email archives@soton.ac.uk
http://www.soton.ac.uk/~papers1/

Archivist: Dr CM Woolgar
Open Mon, Tues, Thurs, Fri 9–5;
  Wed 10–5
Book in advance
Wheelchair access
HMC

**Strathclyde University Archives
(code: 249)**
McCance Building, 16 Richmond
  Street, Glasgow G1 1XQ

Tel 0141 548 2397
Fax 0141 552 0775
Email suarchives@mis.strath.ac.uk
http://www.strath.ac.uk/Departments/
  Archives/

Archivist: Dr James McGrath
Open Term Mon–Fri 9.15–4.45
Book in advance
Wheelchair access
Research service

**Sussex University Library
Manuscript Collections (code: 181)**
Falmer, Brighton BN1 9QL

Tel 01273 606755 ext 3489
Fax 01273 678441
Email e.t.inglis@sussex.ac.uk
http://www.susx.ac.uk/Units/library/
  manuscript/

Librarian: Mr AN Peasgood
Assistant Librarian with
  responsibility for manuscripts:
  Ms Elizabeth Inglis
Open Mon–Wed 9.15–5
Letter of introduction required
Book in advance
Wheelchair access

Mass-Observation Archive
(code: 1995)

Tel 01273 678157
Fax 01273 678441
Email moa@sussex.ac.uk
http://www.sussex.ac.uk/libary/
   massobs/

Archivist: Ms Dorothy Sheridan
Open Mon–Wed 9.15–5
Letter of introduction required
Book at least one week in advance.

Tate Gallery Archive (code: 70)
20 John Islip Street, London SW1P
   4RG

Tel 0171 887 8831
   (020 7887 8831)
Fax 0171 887 8007
   (020 7887 8007)
http://www.tate.org.uk/gall/london/
   menulon.htm

Head of Archive and Registry:
   Mrs Jennifer Booth
Open Tues, Thurs, Fri 10–1, 2–5.30
Letters of introduction (2) required
Book in advance
No wheelchair access
P

**University of Kent at Canterbury
Library (code: 1089)**
Canterbury CT2 7NU

Tel 01227 764000 ext 7609
Fax 01227 823984
Email sac1@ukc.ac.uk
http://libservb.ukc.ac.uk/library/

Special Collections Librarian:
   Mrs S Crabtree
Open Mon–Fri 9–5
Proof of ID and letter of introduction
   required
Book in advance
Wheelchair access

**University of Wales, Bangor,
Department of Manuscripts
(code: 222)**
Bangor LL57 2DG

Tel 01248 351151 ext 2966
Fax 01248 382979
Email iss177@bangor.ac.uk
http://www.llgc.org.uk/cac/
   cac0024.htm

Archivist and Keeper of
   Manuscripts: Mr Tomos Roberts
Open Mon–Fri 9–5; Wed to 9 in term
Book in advance
Wheelchair access
P M&T

**University of Wales Swansea
Library (code: 217)**
Library and Information Centre,
   Singleton Park, Swansea SA2 8PP

Tel 01792 295021
Fax 01792 295851
Email library@swansea.ac.uk
http://www.swan.ac.uk/lis/archives/

Archivist: Ms Elisabeth Bennett
Open Mon–Fri 9.15–12.45, 2–5.
   Tues 6–9.30 in term
Book in advance
Wheelchair access

**Victoria & Albert Museum, National
Art Library (code: 72)**
Cromwell Road, London SW7 2RL

Tel 0171 938 8315
(020 7938 8315)
Fax 0171 938 8461
(020 7938 8461)
http://www.nal.vam.ac.uk/

Curator of Manuscripts: Dr Rowan
   Watson
Open Tues–Sat 10–5. Closed for
   three weeks from August bank
   holiday
Readers ticket required (letter of
   introduction in first instance)
Special arrangements for wheelchairs

N.B. The records of the V&A itself
   are located at Blythe House with
   the Archive of Art and Design

**Victoria & Albert Museum, National
Art Library, Archive of Art and
Design (code: 73)**
Blythe House, 23 Blythe Road,
   London W14 0QF

Tel 0171 603 1514
(020 7603 1514)
Fax 0171 602 0980
(020 7602 0980)
http://www.nal.vam.ac.uk/nalaad.html

Curator in charge: Ms Serena Kelly
Open Tues–Thurs 10–4.30. Closed
   for three weeks after August bank
   holiday
Proof of ID required
Book in advance
No wheelchair access

**Victoria & Albert Museum, Theatre
Museum (code: 71)**
1E Tavistock Street, Covent Garden,
   London WC2E 7PA

Tel 0171 836 7891
(020 7836 7891)
Fax 0171 836 5148
(020 7836 5148)
http://www.vam.ac.uk/

Head of Library and Information
   Services: Ms Claire Hudson
Open: Tues–Fri 10.30–1, 2–4.30
Book in advance (2–3 weeks)
Wheelchair access

**Warwick University Modern
Records Centre (code: 152)**
University Library, University of
   Warwick, Coventry CV4 7AL

Tel 01203 524219
(024 7652 4219)
Fax 01203 572988
(024 7657 2988)
Email archives@warwick.ac.uk
http://www.warwick.ac.uk/services/
   library/mrc/mrc.html

Archivist: Mrs Christine Woodland
Open Mon–Thurs 9–1, 1.30–5;
   Fri 9–1, 1.30–4: Closed one week at
   Easter
Book in advance
Wheelchair access
Research service
HMC

**Wellcome Institute for the History of
Medicine, Department of Western
Manuscripts (code: 120)**
183 Euston Road, London NW1 2BE

Tel 0171 611 8582
(020 7611 8582)
Fax 0171 611 8703
(020 7611 8703)
Email library@wellcome.ac.uk
http://www.wellcome.ac.uk/library/

Curator of Western Manuscripts:
  Dr RK Aspin
Open Mon, Wed, Fri 9.45–5.15; Tues,
  Thurs 9.45–7.15; Sat 9.45–1
Readers ticket required
Wheelchair access

Wellcome Institute for the History of Medicine, Contemporary Medical Archives Centre (code: 121)

Tel 0171 611 8483
  (020 7611 8483)
Fax 0171 611 8703
  (020 7611 8703)
Email cmac@wellcome.ac.uk
http://www.wellcome.ac.uk/library/

Archivist: Miss Julia Sheppard
Open Mon, Wed, Fri 9.45–5.15; Tues,
  Thurs 9.45–7.30; Sat 9.45–1
Readers ticket required
Book in advance
Wheelchair access

Westminster Abbey Muniment Room and Library (code: 119)
London SW1P 3PA

Tel 0171 222 5152 ext 228
  (020 7222 5152 ext 228)
Fax 0171 233 2072
  (020 7233 2072)
Email library@westminster-abbey.org
http://www.westminster-abbey.org/

Keeper of the Muniments: Dr Richard
  Mortimer
Open Mon–Fri 10–1, 2–4.45
Letter of introduction required
Book in advance
Special arrangements fo wheelchairs
P M&T

Westminster Diocesan Archives (code: 122)
16a Abingdon Road, Kensington,
  London W8 6AF

Tel 0171 938 3580
  (020 7938 3580)

Archivist: Revd Ian Dickie
Open Tues–Fri 10–1, 2–5
Proof of ID required
Book in advance
No wheelchair access

Westminster University Archives (code: 1753)
Information Systems and Library
  Services, 4–12 Little Titchfield
  Street, London W1P 7FW

Tel 0171 911 5000 ext 2524
  (020 7911 5000 ext 2524)
Fax 1071 911 5894
  (020 7911 5894)
Email archive@westminster.ac.uk

Archivist: Mrs Brenda Weeden
Open by appointment
Proof of identity required
Wheelchair access

Working Class Movement Library (code: 1008)
Jubilee House, 51 The Crescent,
  Salford, Manchester M5 4WX

Tel 0161 736 3601
Fax 0161 737 4115
Email enquiries@wcml.org.uk
http://www.wcml.org.uk/

Librarian: Mr Alain Kahan
Open Tues, Thurs, Fri 10–5;
  Wed 10–9; alternate Sun 2–5
Proof of ID required
Book in advance
Wheelchair access

York Minster Archives (code: 195)
York Minster Library, Dean's Park,
  York YO1 7JQ

Tel 01904 611118
Fax 01904 611119
Email archives@yorkminster.org
http://www.yorkminster.org/

Archivist: Mrs L Hampson
Open Mon–Thurs 9–5; Fri 9–12
Proof of ID required
Book in advance
Wheelchair access
Research service
P

**York University, Borthwick Institute
  of Historical Research (code: 193)**
St Anthony's Hall, Peasholme Green,
  York YO1 7PW

Tel 01904 642315
http://www.york.ac.uk/inst/bihr/

Director: Professor David Smith
Open Mon–Fri 9.30–12.50; 2–4.50.
  Closed one week at Easter
Book in advance
Special arrangements for wheelchairs
Research service
HMC P D (York)

Part 2: Local Repositories in Great Britain

Entries in this part appear in alphabetical order of first geographical reference, i.e. Corporation of London appears under London; Royal Institution of Cornwall appears under Cornwall; West Yorkshire Archive Service appears under Yorkshire. The one local repository without a geographical designation – the Shakespeare Birthplace Trust – appears alphabetically.

ENGLAND

Barking and Dagenham Public Libraries, Valence House Museum (code: 350)
Becontree Avenue, Dagenham, Essex
  RM8 3HT

Tel 0181 227 5293
  (020 8227 5293)
Fax 0181 227 5293
  (020 8227 5293)
Email fm019@viscount.org.uk
http://www.earl.org.uk/partners/
  barking/index.html

Heritage Services Manager: Ms
  Susan Curtis
Open Tues–Fri 9.30–1, 2–4.30;
  Sat 10–4
Proof of ID required
Book in advance
Wheelchair access

Barnet Local Studies and Archives Department (code: 77)
Hendon Catholic Social Centre,
  Chapel Walk, Egerton Gardens,
  London NW4 4BE
Correspondence address: Hendon
  Library, The Burroughs, Hendon,
  London NW4 4BQ

Tel 020 8359 2628
Fax 020 8359 2885
Borough Archivist: post vacant
Open Tues, Wed, Sat 9.30–12.30,
  1.30–5; Thurs 12.30–7.30
Book in advance
Special arrangements for wheelchairs
M&T

Barnsley Archive Service (code: 196)
Central Library, Shambles Street,
  Barnsley S70 2JF

Tel 01226 773950/773938
Fax 01226 773955
Email Archives@barnsley.ac.uk

Archives and Local Studies Officer:
  Mrs L Whitworth-Cox
Open Mon, Wed 9.30–6;
  Tues, Fri 9.30–5.30; Sat 9.30–1
Book in advance
Wheelchair access

Bath and North East Somerset Record Office (code: 1)
Guildhall, High Street, Bath BA1
  5AW

Tel 01225 477421
Fax 01225 477439
Email Colin_Johnston@bathnes.
 gov.uk

Archivist: Mr CA Johnston
Open Mon 9–1, 2–8;
 Tues–Thurs 9–1, 2–5;
 Fri 9–1, 2–4.30
Wheelchair access
P M&T

N.B. Records relating to parts of the
 historic county of Somerset are
 collected by Somerset Record
 Office where these are additions to
 existing series in their keeping.

**Bedfordshire and Luton Archives
and Record Service (code: 4)**
The Record Office, County Hall,
 Cauldwell Street, Bedford MK42
 9AP

Tel 01234 228833/228777
Fax 01234 228854
Email archive@csd.bedfordshire.
 gov.uk
http://www.bedfordshire.gov.uk/

County Archivist: Mr Kevin Ward
Open Mon–Fri 9–1, 2–5 (opens at 10
 first Thurs in month)
No wheelchair access
Research Service
HMC P D (St Albans: parish records
 of Bedford archdeaconry)

Berkshire Record Office (code: 5)
Shire Hall, Shinfield Park, Reading
 RG2 9XD

Tel 0118 901 5132
Fax 0118 901 5131
Email archives@reading.gov.uk

County Archivist: Dr Peter Durrant
Open Tues–Wed 9–5; Thurs 9–9; Fri
 9–4.30. Closed two weeks in
 October/November
Member of the CARN scheme
Book in advance
Wheelchair access
Research service
P M&T D (Oxford: Berkshire
 archdeaconry)

N.B. Will be moving to Castle Hill,
 Reading, in Spring 2000.

**Berwick-upon-Tweed Record Office
(code: 757)**
Council Offices, Wallace Green,
 Berwick upon Tweed TD15 1ED

Tel 01289 330044 ext 230
Fax 01289 330540
Email lb@berwick-upon-tweed.
 gov.uk

Borough Archivist: Mrs LA Bankier
Open Wed, Thurs 9.30–1, 2–5
Book in advance
Wheelchair access
Research service
P

**Bexley Local Studies and Archives
Centre (code: 79)**
Hall Place, Bourne Road, Bexley DA5
 1PQ

Tel 01322 526574 ext 217/8
Fax 01322 522921
Email bexlibs@dial.pipex.com
http://www.bexley.gov.uk/

Local Studies Manager:
Mr Stuart Bligh
Open Mon–Sat 9–5 (in winter 9 to
dusk)
Wheelchair access
D (Rochester: parish records of Erith
and Sidcup deaneries)

Birmingham City Archives (code: 143)

Central Library, Chamberlain Square,
Birmingham B3 3HQ

Tel 0121 303 4217
Fax 0121 212 9397
http://www.birmingham.gov.uk/

Central Library Manager, Archives,
Local Studies and History:
Mr NW Kingsley
Senior Archivist: Sian Roberts
Open Mon, Tues, Thurs–Sat 9–5
Member of CARN scheme
Special arrangements for wheelchairs
Research service
P M&T D (Birmingham)

Bolton Archive and Local Studies Service (code: 125)

Central Library, Civic Centre, Le
Mans Crescent, Bolton BL1 1SE

Tel 01204 522311 ext 2179
Fax 01204 363224

Borough Archivist: Mr TK Campbell
Open Tues, Thurs 9.30–7.30; Wed,
Fri 9.30–5.309; Sat 9.30–5
Book in advance
Wheelchair access
P

Brent Community History Library and Archive (code: 80)

Cricklewood Library, 152 Olive Road,
Cricklewood, London NW2 6UY

Tel 0181 937 3540
(020 8937 3540
Fax 0181 480 5211
(020 8450 5211)
http://www.brent.gov.uk/

Library Manager: Mr Stephen Allen
Open Mon 1–5; Tues 10–5;
Thurs 1–8; Sat 10–5
Proof of ID required
Book in advance
Wheelchair access

Bristol Record Office (code: 2)

'B' Bond Warehouse, Smeaton Road,
Bristol BS1 6XN

Tel 0117 922 5692
Fax 0117 922 4236
http://www.bristol-city.gov.uk/

City Archivist: Mr John Williams
Open Mon–Thurs 9.30–4.45. First
Thurs each month to 8 by
appointment (suspended until Sept
1999). Closed last two weeks in
January
Book in advance
Wheelchair access
Research service
P M&T D (Bristol)

Bromley Public Libraries, Local Studies and Archives (code: 81)

Central Library, High Street, Bromley
BR1 1EX

Tel 0181 460 9955 ext 261
(020 8460 9955 ext 261)
Fax 0181 313 9975
(020 8313 9975)
http://www.bromley.gov.uk/

Archivist: Miss E Silverthorne
Open Mon, Wed, Fri 9.30–6; Tues,
  Thurs 9.30–8; Sat 9.30–5
Book in advance
Wheelchair access
P D (Rochester: parish records of
  Beckenham, Bromley and Orpington
  deaneries)

Buckinghamshire Records and Local Studies Service (code: 8)
County Hall, Aylesbury HP20 1UU

Tel 01296 382587
Fax 01296 382274
Email archives@buckscc.gov.uk
http://www.buckscc.gov.uk/leisure/
  archives/

County Archivist: Mr Roger
  Bettridge
Open Mon–Thurs 9–5.15; Fri 9–4.45.
  First Thurs in month to 7.45 by
  appointment
Member of the CARN scheme
Book in advance
Wheelchair access
Research service
P M&T D (Oxford: Buckingham
  archdeaconry)

Bury Archive Service (code: 126)
1st Floor, Derby Hall Annexe, Edwin
  Street (off Crompton Street), Bury
  BL9 0AS

Tel 0161 797 6697
Fax 0161 253 5915
Email information@bury.gov.uk
http://www.bury.gov.uk/

Archivist: Mr KJ Mulley
Open Mon–Fri 10–1, 2–5. First Sat in
  each month 10–1
Member of CARN scheme
Book in advance, except Tues
Special arrangements for wheelchairs

Cambridgeshire County Record Office, Cambridge (code: 10)
Shire Hall, Castle Hill, Cambridge CB3
  0AP

Tel 01223 717281
Fax 01223 717201
Email county.records.cambridge
  @camcnty.gov.uk
http://www.camcnty.gov.uk/

County Archivist: Mrs EA Stazicker
Deputy County Archivist:
  Dr Philip Saunders
Open Tues–Thurs 9–12.45, 1.45–5.15;
  Fri 9–12.45, 1.45–4.15; Tues to 9 by
  appointment
Member of CARN scheme
Book in advance
Wheelchair access
Research service
P M&T D (Ely: parish records of Ely
  archdeaconry and Ely and March
  deaneries)

Cambridgeshire County Record Office, Huntingdon (code: 11)
Grammar School Walk, Huntingdon
  PE18 6LF

Tel 01480 375842
Fax 01480 459563
Email
  county.records.hunts@camcnty.gov.uk
http://www.camcnty.gov.uk/

Senior Archivist: Mr Alan Akeroyd
Open Tues–Thurs 9–12.45, 1.45–5.15;
  Fri 9–12.45, 1.45–4.15; second Sat in
  month 9–12
Member of the CARN scheme
No wheelchair access
Research service
P M&T D (Ely: parish records of
  Huntingdon archdeaconry)

Camden Local Studies and Archives Centre (code: 784)
Holborn Library, 32–38 Theobalds Road, London WC1X 8PA

Tel 0171 413 6342
(020 7413 6342)
Fax 0171 413 6284
(020 7413 6284)

Local Studies Manager:
Mr RG Knight
Open Mon, Thurs 10–7; Tues 10–6;
Fri 10–1; Sat 10–1, 2–5
Book in advance
Wheelchair access

Cheshire Record Office (code: 17)
Duke Street, Chester CH1 1RL

Tel 01244 602574
Fax 01244 603812
Email recordoffice@cheshire.gov.uk
http://www.cheshire.gov.uk/recoff/
home.htm

County Archivist: Mr Jonathan Pepler
Open Mon–Fri 9.15–4.45, second Wed in month to 8.30; fourth Sat in month 9–12
Member of the CARN scheme
Book in advance
Wheelchair access
Research service
P M&T D (Chester. Liverpool: parish records of Warrington and Farnworth deaneries)

Chester Archives (code: 18)
Town Hall, Chester CH1 2HJ

Tel 01244 402110
Fax 01244 312243
Email j.gregson@chestercc.gov.uk
http://www.chestercc.gov.uk/
heritage/archives/home.html

Public Services Coordinator: Mrs Jacqui Halewood
Open Mon, Tues, Thurs, Fri 10–4
Member of the CARN scheme
Wheelchair access
Research service
P M&T

Cornwall Record Office (code: 21)
County Hall, Truro TR1 3AY

Tel 01872 273698/323127
Fax 01872 270340

County Archivist: Mrs Christine North
Open Tues–Thurs 9.30–1, 2–5;
Fri 9–4.30; Sat 9–12 except preceeding bank holidays.
Closed first two weeks in December
Member of the CARN scheme
Book in advance
Wheelchair access
Research service
P M&T D (Truro)

Royal Institution of Cornwall (code: 22)
Royal Cornwall Museum, River Street, Truro TR1 2SJ
Correspondence address: The Courtney Library, Royal Institution of Cornwall, River Street, Truro TR1 2SJ

Tel 01872 272205
Fax 01872 240514
http://www.cornwall-online.co.uk/ric/

Librarian: Ms Angela Broome
Open Mon–Sat 10–1, 2–5
Book in advance
Wheelchair access
Research service

Coventry City Archives (code: 144)
Mandela House, Bayley Lane,
  Coventry CV1 5RG

Tel 01203 832418
  (024 7683 2418)
Fax 01203 832421
  (024 7683 2421)
Email coventryarchives@discover.
  co.uk

City Archivist: Mr Roger Vaughan
Open Mon 9.30–8; Tues–Fri 9.30–
  4.45
Member of the CARN scheme
Book in advance for microform
  facilities and on Monday evenings
Wheelchair access
Research service
P M&T

**Croydon Archives Service
(code: 352)**
Central Library, Croydon Clocktower,
  Katharine Street, Croydon CR9 1ET

Tel 0181 760 5400 ext 1112
  (020 8760 5400 ext 1112)
Fax 0181 253 1004
  (020 8253 1004)
Email dparr@library.croydon.gov.uk
http://www.croydon.gov.uk/

Archivist: Mr Steve Griffiths
Open Mon 9–7; Tues, Wed, Fri 9–6;
  Thurs 9.30–6; Sat 9–5
Book in advance
Wheelchair access

**Cumbria Record Office, Carlisle
Headquarters (code: 23)**
The Castle, Carlisle CA3 8UR

Tel 01228 607285
Fax 01288 607274
Email carlisle.record.office@
  cumbriacc.gov.uk

County Archivist:
  Mr Jim Grisenthwaite
Assistant County Archivist: Mr
  David Bowcock
Open Mon–Fri 9–5
Member of the CARN scheme
Wheelchair access
Research service
P M&T D (Carlisle)

N.B. A website is under construction,
  URL yet to be decided. Check
  ARCHON for details.

**Cumbria Record Office and Local
Studies Library, Barrow (code: 25)**
140 Duke Street, Barrow-in-Furness
LA14 1XW

Tel 01229 894363
Fax 01229 894371
Email barrow.record.office@
  cumbriacc.gov.uk

Area Archivist: Mr ACJ Jones
Open Mon–Fri 9–5; Wed eves and
  Sat by appointment
Member of CARN cheme
Wheelchair access
Research service
P M&T D (Carlisle)

**Cumbria Record Office, Kendal
(code: 24)**
County Offices, Kendal LA9 4RQ

Tel 01539 773540
Fax 01539 773439
Email kendall.record.office
  @cumbriacc.gov.uk

Assistant County Archivist:
  Ms Anne Rowe
Open Mon–Fri 9–5
Member of the CARN scheme
Wheelchair access
Research service
P M&T D (Carlisle: Bradford parish
  records)

**Cumbria Record Office and Local
Studies Library, Whitehaven**
Scotch Street, Whitehaven CA28 7BJ

Tel 01946 852920
Fax 01946 852919
Email whrec@dial.pipex.com.

Area Archivist: Mr Peter J Eyre
Open Mon–Fri 9.30–5, Wed to 7.
  Open Sat 9–1 by appointment
Member of CARN scheme
Wheelchair access
Research service
HMC P D (Carlisle)

Derbyshire Record Office (code: 26)
New Street, Matlock
Correspondence address: County
  Hall, Matlock DE4 3AG

Tel 01629 585347
Fax 01629 57611

County Archivist:
  Dr Margaret O'Sullivan
Open Mon–Fri 9.30–4.45
Proof of ID required
Book in advance
Wheelchair access
Research service
HMC P D (Derby)

Devon Record Office (code: 27)
Castle Street, Exeter EX4 3PU
Tel 01392 384253
Fax 01392 384256
Email devrec@devon-cc.gov.uk
http://www.devon-cc.gov.uk/dro/

County Archivist: Mr John Draisey
Open Mon–Thurs 10–5; Fri 10–4.30
Member of CARN scheme
A fee may be payable
Wheelchair access
Research service
P M&T D (Exeter)

**North Devon Record Office
(code: 821)**
North Devon Library and Record
  Office, Tuly Street, Barnstaple EX31
  1EL

Tel 01271 388608
Fax 01271 388608
http://www.devon-cc.gov.uk/dro/

Senior Archivist:
  Mr Timothy Wormleighton
Open Mon, Tues, Thurs, Fri 9.30–5;
  Wed 9.30–4; two Sat per month
  9.30–4
Member of the CARN scheme
Book in advance
A fee may be payable
Wheelchair access
Research service
P M&T D (Exeter: Barnstaple
  archdeaconry)

**Doncaster Archives Department
(code: 197)**
King Edward Road, Balby, Doncaster
  DN4 0NA

Tel 01302 859811

Principal Archivist: Dr BJ Barber
Open Mon–Fri 9–12.45, 2–4.45
Readers ticket required
Book in advance
Wheelchair access
Research service
P M&T D (Sheffield: Doncaster
  archdeaconry)

Dorset Record Office (code: 31)
Bridport Road, Dorchester DT1 1RP

Tel 01305 250550
Fax 01305 257184
Email dcc_archives@dorset-cc.
  gov.uk
http://www.dorset-cc.gov.uk/
  records.htm

County Archivist: Mr Hugh Jaques
Open Mon, Tues, Thurs, Fri 9–5;
  Wed 10–5; Sat 9.30–12.30
Proof of ID required
Book in advance
Wheelchair access
Research service
HMC P D (Salisbury: parish records
  of Dorset and Sherborne
  archdeaconries)

**Dudley Archives and Local History
Service (code: 145)**
Mount Pleasant Street, Coseley,
  Dudley WV14 9JR

Tel 01384 812770
Fax 01384 812770
Email archives.pls
  @mbc.dudley.gov.uk
http://www.dudley.gov.uk/

Archivist: Mrs KH Atkins
Open Tues, Wed, Fri 9–5, Thurs
  9.30–7, first and third Sat in month
  9.30–12.30
Readers ticket required (proof of ID
  in first instance)
Book in advance
Wheelchair access
Research service
P M&T D (Worcester: parish
  registers for the deaneries of
  Dudley, Hinley and Stourbridge)

**Durham County Record Office
(code: 32)**
County Hall, Durham DH1 5UL

Tel 0191 383 3253/3474
Fax 0191 383 4500
http://www.durham.gov.uk/

County Archivist: Miss J Gill
Open Mon, Tues, Thurs 8.45–4.45;
  Wed 8.45–8; Fri 8.45–4.15
Book in advance
Wheelchair access
Research service
P M&T D (Durham. Ripon: parish
  records)

**Ealing Local History Centre
(code: 1158)**
Central Library, 103 Ealing Broadway
  Centre, London W5 5JY

Tel 0181 567 3656 ext 37
  (020 8567 3656 ext 37)
Fax 0181 840 2351
  (020 8840 2351)
Email localhistory@hotmail.com

Local History Archivist:
  Mr Jonathon Oates
Open Tues, Thurs 9.30–7.45; Wed,
  Fri, Sat 9.30–5
Wheelchair access

**Enfield Local History Unit
(code: 353)**
Southgate Town Hall, Green Lanes,
Palmers Green, London N13 4XD

Tel 0181 379 2724
(020 8379 2724)
Fax 0181 379 2761
(020 8379 2761)

Local History Officer: Mr GC Dalling
Open Mon–Sat 9–5
Book in advance
Wheelchair access

Essex Record Office (code: 37)
County Hall, Chelmsford CM1 1LX

Tel 01245 430067
Fax 01245 430085
Email ero.enquiry@essexcc.gov.uk
http://www.essexcc.gov.uk/heritage/
fs_recof.htm

County Archivist: Mr Ken Hall
Open Mon 10–8.45; Tues–Thurs
9.15–5.15; Fri 9.15–4.15;
Sat 9.15–4.15
Member of the CARN scheme
Book in advance
Wheelchair access
Research service
P M&T D (Chelmsford)

**Essex Record Office, Colchester and
North-East Essex Branch (code: 38)**
Stanwell House, Stanwell Street,
Colchester C02 7DL

Tel 01206 572099
Fax 01206 574541
http://www.essexcc.gov.uk/heritage/
fs_recof.htm

Branch Archivist: Mr PRJ Coverley
Open Mon 10–5.15 (8.45 on second
Mon in month), Tues–Thurs
9.15–5.15; Fri 9.15–4.15
Member of the CARN scheme
Book in advance
Wheelchair access
P M&T D (Chelmsford: NE Essex
parish records)

**Essex Record Office, Southend
Branch (code: 39)**
Central Library, Victoria Avenue,
Southend-on-Sea SS2 6EX

Tel 01702 464278
Fax 01702 464252
http://www.essexcc.gov.uk/heritage/
fs_recof.htm

Archivist in charge: Mr Julian Reid
Open Mon 10–5.15; Tues–Thurs
9.15–5.15; Fri 9.15–4.15
Member of the CARN scheme
Book in advance
Wheelchair access
Research service

**Finsbury Library, Local History
Collection (code: 1157)**
245 St John Street, London EC1V
4NB

Tel 0171 619 7988
(020 7619 7988)
Fax 0171 278 8821
(020 7278 8821)

Reference Librarian:
Mr David Withey
Open Mon, Thurs 9.30–8; Tues,
Sat 9.30–5; Fri 9.30–1
Book in advance
Special arrangements for wheelchairs
Research service

Gateshead Central Library, Local Studies Collection (code: 185)
Prince Consort Road, Gateshead NE8 4LN

Tel 0191 477 3478
Fax 0191 477 7454
Email local@gateslib.demon.co.uk
http://www.swinhope.demon.co.uk/
  genuki/DUR/GatesheadLib/

Local Studies Librarian:
  Miss E Carnaffin
Open Mon, Tues, Thurs, Fri 9–7;
  Wed 9–5; Sat 9–1
Wheelchair access
M&T

Gloucestershire Record Office (code: 40)
Clarence Row, Alvin Street,
  Gloucester GL1 3DW

Tel 01452 425295
Fax 01452 426378
Email records@gloscc.gov.uk
http://www.gloscc.gov.uk/pubserv/
  gcc/corpserv/archives/index.htm

County Archivist: Mr DJH Smith
Open Mon 10–5; Tues, Wed, Fri 9–5;
  Thurs 9–8. Closed first two weeks
  in December
Readers ticket required (proof of ID
  in first instance)
A fee may be payable
Wheelchair access
Research service
P M&T D (Gloucester)

Greenwich Local History Library (code: 83)
Woodlands, 90 Mycenae Road,
  Blackheath, London SE3 7SE

Tel 0181 858 4631
(020 8858 4631)
Fax 0181 293 4721
(020 8293 4721)

Local History Librarian:
  Mr Julian Watson
Open Mon, Tues 9–5.30; Thurs 9–8;
  Sat 9–5
Book in advance for microform
  facilities
No wheelchair access
P

Hackney Archives Department (code: 84)
43 De Beauvoir Road, London N1 5SQ

Tel 0171 241 2886
(020 7241 2886)
Fax 0171 241 6688
(020 7241 6688)
Email archives@hackney.gov.uk
http://www.hackney.gov.uk/

Archivist: Mr David Mander
Open Mon, Tues, Thurs 9.30–1, 2–5;
  first and third Sat in month 9.30–1,
  2–5
Book in advance
Wheelchair access
Research service
P

Hammersmith and Fulham Archives and Local History Centre (code: 85)
The Lilla Huset, 191 Talgarth Road,
  London W6 8BJ

Tel 0181 741 5159
(020 8741 5159)
Fax 0181 741 4882
(020 8741 4882)
http://www.lbhf.gov.uk/index3.htm

Borough Archivist: Ms Jane Kimber
Open Mon 9.30–8; Tues, and first Sat
in month 9.30–1; Thurs 9.30–4.30
Book in advance
Wheelchair access
P M&T

Hampshire Record Office (code: 41)
Sussex Street, Winchester S023 8TH

Tel 01962 846154
Fax 01962 878681
Email sadeax@hants.gov.uk
http://www.hants.gov.uk:80/record-
office/index.html

County Archivist:
  Miss Rosemary Dunhill
Open Mon–Fri 9–7; Sat 9–4
Member of the CARN scheme
Book in advance for microform
  facilities
Wheelchair access
Research service
P M&T D (Winchester, except
  Southampton. Portsmouth: parish
  records of Petersfield and Bishops
  Waltham deaneries)

Haringey Archive Service (code: 86)
Bruce Castle Museum, Lordship
  Lane, London N17 8NU

Tel 0181 808 8772
  (020 8808 8772)
Fax 0181 808 4118
  (020 8808 4118)

Local History Officer: Ms Rita Read
Open by appointment only
No wheelchair access

Harrow Reference Library
(code: 1102)
PO Box 4, Civic Centre, Station Road,
  Harrow HA1 2UU
Tel 0181 424 1056
  (020 8424 1056)
Fax 0181 424 1971
  (020 8424 1971)

Local History Librarian:
  Mr R W Thomson
Open Mon, Tues, Thurs 9.30–8;
  Fri 9.30–1; Sat 9–5
Wheelchair access

Herefordshire Record Office
(code: 44)
The Old Barracks, Harold Street,
  Hereford HR1 2QX

Tel 01432 265441
Fax 01432 370248

Head of Repository:
  Miss DS Hubbard
Open Mon 10–4.45; Tues–Thurs
  9.15–4.45; Fri 9.15–4
Member of the CARN scheme
Book in advance for microform
  facilities
Special arrangements for wheelchairs
Research service
P M&T D (Hereford)

Hertfordshire Archives and Local
Studies (code: 46)
County Hall, Hertford SG13 8EJ

Tel 01992 555105
Fax 01992 555113
Email hals@hertscc.gov.uk
http://hertslib.hertscc.gov.uk/
  recthome.htm

County Archivist: post vacant
Open Mon, Wed, Thurs 9.30–5.30;
 Tues 10–8; Fri 9.30–4.30; Sat 9–1
Member of the CARN scheme
Wheelchair access
Research service
P M&T D (St Albans)

Hillingdon Local Heritage Service (code: 354)
Central Library, 14–15 High Street,
 Uxbridge UB8 1HD

Tel 01895 250702
Fax 01895 239794

Local Heritage Coordinator:
 Mrs C Cotton
Open Mon 9.30–8; Tues–Thurs
 1–5.30; Fri 10–5.30; Sat 9.30–12, 1–4
Book in advance
Wheelchair access

Hounslow Reference Library (code: 356)
Hounslow Library Centre, 24 Treaty
 Centre, High Street, Hounslow TW3
 1ES

Tel 0181 570 0622 ext 7892
 (020 8570 0622 ext 7892)
Fax 0181 569 4330
 (020 8569 4330)

Senior Officer, Heritage Services:
 Miss Andrea Cameron
Open [hours due to change]
Proof of ID required
Book in advance
Wheelchair access
Research service

Hull City Archives (code: 49)
79 Lowgate, Kingston upon Hull HU1
 1HN

Tel 01482 615102/615110
Fax 01482 613051

Archivist: Mr GW Oxley
Open Tues, Thurs 9–12.15, 1.30–4.45;
 Wed 9–12.15; Fri 9–12.15, 1.30–4.15.
 Municipal offices (outstore) Wed
 1.45–4.30
Book in advance
Wheelchair access to municipal
 offices only
Research service (via City Library's
 Family History Centre)
P M&T

Isle of Wight County Record Office (code: 189)
26 Hillside, Newport P030 2EB

Tel 01983 823820/1
Fax 01983 823820

County Archivist: Mr Richard Smout
Open Mon 9.30–5; Tues–Fri 9–5.
 First Wed each month to 7.30 by
 appointment
Member of CARN scheme
Book in advance for microform
 facilities
Wheelchair access
Research service
P M&T D (Portsmouth: parish
 records of Isle of Wight
 archdeaconry)

Islington Archives (code: 1032)
Islington Central Library, 2 Fieldway
 Crescent, Islington, London N5 1PF

Tel 0171 619 6931/2
 (020 7619 6931/2)
Fax 0171 607 6409
 (020 7607 6409)
Email is.osc.his@dial.pipex.com
http://www.islington.gov.uk/council/
 library/history.htm

Local History Librarian:
Ms Vada Hart
Open Mon, Wed, Thurs 9–8; Tues,
Fri, Sat 9–5
Book in advance
Wheelchair access
Research service

**Kensington and Chelsea Libraries
and Arts Service (code: 87)**
Central Library, Phillimore Walk,
London W8 7RX (Public entrance is
in Hornton Street)

Tel 0171 361 3038
(020 7361 3038)
Fax 0171 361 2976
(020 7361 2976)

Local Studies Librarian:
Mrs Carolyn Starren
Open Tues, Thurs 10–8; Wed 10–1;
Fri 10–5; Sat 10–1, 2–5
Book in advance
Wheelchair access
Research service

**Centre for Kentish Studies
(code: 51)**
Sessions House, County Hall,
Maidstone ME14 1XQ

Tel 01622 694363
Fax 01622 694379
http://www.kent.gov.uk/arts/
archives/

County Archivist:
Miss Patricia Rowsby
Open Tues, Wed, Fri 9–5; Thurs
10–5; second and fourth Sat in
month 9–1. Closed two weeks in
June
Member of the CARN scheme
Book in advance
Wheelchair access
Research service
P M&T D (Rochester: Tonbridge
archdeaconry. Canterbury:
Maidstone archdeaconry)

**East Kent Archive Centre
(code: 2006)**
Enterprise Business Park,
Honeywood Road, Whitfield, Dover
CT16 3EH

Tel 01304 829306

Senior Archivist: Miss Janice Taylor

N.B. Will open in early 2000 for
records transferred from Folkestone
Library and Ramsgate Library.

**Kingston Museum and Heritage
Service (code: 177)**
North Kingston Centre, Richmond
Road, Kingston upon Thames KT2
5PE

Tel 0181 547 6753
(020 8547 6753)
Fax 0181 547 6747
(020 8547 6747)
Email king.mus@rbk.kingston.gov.uk
http://www.kingston.gov.uk/museum/
localhistory.htm

Heritage Officer:
  Mrs Anne McCormack
Archivist: Mrs Jill Lamb
Open Mon, Thurs, Fri 10–5; Tues
  10–7.
Book in advance
No wheelchair access
Research service
P

**Lambeth Archives Department
(code: 88)**
Minet Library, 52 Knatchbull Road,
  London SE5 9QY

Tel 0171 926 6076
  (020 7926 6076)
Fax 0171 926 6080
  (020 7926 6080)

Archives Manager: Mr Jon Newman/
  Ms Sue McKenzie
Open Mon 10.30–7.30, Tues, Thurs
  9.30–5.30; Fri 9.30–1; Sat 9.30–5
Book in advance
Wheelchair access
M&T

Lancashire Record Office (code: 55)
Bow Lane, Preston PR1 2RE

Tel 01772 263039
Fax 01772 263050
Email Bruce.Jackson
  @treas.lancscc.gov.uk
http://www.lancashire.com/lcc/edu/
  ro/

County Archivist: Mr Bruce Jackson
Open Mon 9–5; Tues 9–8.30; Wed,
  Thurs 9–5; Fri 9–4. Closed first
  week in each month
Member of the CARN scheme
Wheelchair access
HMC P D (Blackburn. Bradford:
  parish records of Bowland deanery.
  Liverpool parish records of
  northern deaneries. Chester:
  Richmond archdeaconry)

**The Record Office for
Leicestershire, Leicester and
Rutland (code: 56)**
Long Street, Wigston Magna,
  Leicester LE18 2AH

Tel 0116 257 1080
Fax 0116 257 1120

County Archivist: Mr CW Harrison
Open Mon, Tues, Thurs 9.15–5;
  Wed 9.15–7.30; Fri 9.15–4.45;
  Sat 9.15–12.15. Closed first week in
  October
Member of the CARN scheme
Wheelchair access
Research service
P M&T D (Leicester. Peterborough:
  Rutland parish records)

**Lewisham Local Studies Centre
(code: 89)**
Lewisham Library, 199–201 Lewisham
  High Street, London SE1 6LG

Tel 0181 297 0682
  (020 8297 0682)
Fax 0181 297 1169
  (020 8297 1169)
Email local.studies@lewisham.gov.uk
http://www.lewisham.gov.uk/

Archivist: Ms Jean Wait
Open Mon 10–5; Tues, Thurs 9–8;
   Fri, Sat 9–5. Closed first two weeks
   in December
Book in advance
Wheelchair access
HMC P D (Southwark: parish records
   of East and West Lewisham
   deaneries)

Lincolnshire Archives (code: 57)
St Rumbold Street, Lincoln LN2 5AB

Tel 01522 526204
Fax 01522 530047
Email archives
   @lincsdoc.demon.co.uk
http://www.lincs-archives.com/

Area Service Manager:
   Mr CPC Johnson
Principal Keeper: Mrs SM Payne
Open Mon 1–7 (1–5 in Nov–Feb);
   Tues–Fri 9–5; Sat 9–4
Readers ticket required (proof of ID
   in first instance)
Book in advance
Wheelchair access
Research service
P M&T D (Lincoln)

**North East Lincolnshire Archives
(code: 48)**
Town Hall, Town Hall Square,
   Grimsby DN31 1HX

Tel 01472 323585
Fax 01472 323582

Archivist: Mr John Wilson
Open Mon–Fri 9.30–12, 1–4.30
Book in advance for microform
   facilities
Wheelchair access
Research service
P M&T

**Liverpool Record Office and Local
History Service (code: 138)**
Central Library, William Brown Street,
   Liverpool L3 8EW

Tel 0151 233 5817
Fax 0151 207 1342
Email recoffice.central.library@
   liverpool.gov.uk
http://www.liverpool.gov.uk/

Head of Local Studies and Archives:
   Mr David Stoker
Open Mon–Thurs 9–7.30; Fri 9–5;
   Sat 10–4. Closed third and fourth
   weeks in June
Readers ticket required
Book in advance for microform
   facilities
There is an advance booking fee for
   microform readers
Wheelchair access
P M&T D (Liverpool)

**Corporation of London, London
Metropolitan Archives (code: 74)**
40 Northampton Road, London EC1R
   0HB

Tel 0171 332 3820
   (020 7332 3820)
Fax 0171 833 9136
   (020 7833 9136)
Minicom 0171 278 8703
   (020 7278 8703)
Email LMA@ms.corpoflondon.
   gov.uk

Head Archivist: Dr Deborah Jenkins
Open Mon–Fri 9.30–4.45; Tues,
   Thurs to 7.30. Closed first two
   weeks in November
Wheelchair access
Research service
P M&T D (London. Southwark.
   Guildford)

Corporation of London, Guildhall Library (code: 76)
Aldermanbury, London EC2P 2EJ

Tel 0171 332 1862/3
  (020 7332 1862/3)
Fax 0171 600 3384
  (020 7600 3384)
Email Manuscripts.Guildhall@
  ms.corpoflondon.gov.uk
http://ihr.sas.ac.uk/gh/

Keeper of Manuscripts:
  Mr SGH Freeth
Open Mon–Sat 9.30–4.45
Wheelchair access
P M&T D (London)

Corporation of London Records Office (code: 75)
PO Box 270, Guildhall, London EC2P 2EJ

Tel 0171 332 1251
  (020 7332 1251)
Fax 0171 332 1119
  (020 7332 1119)
http://www.corpoflondon.gov.uk/

City Archivist: Mr JR Sewell
Open Mon–Fri 9.30–4.45
Proof of ID required
Readers wishing to look at rate books
  should book in advance
Special arrangements for wheelchairs
P M&T

Greater Manchester County Record Office (code: 124)
56 Marshall Street, New Cross,
  Manchester M4 5FU

Tel 0161 832 5284
Fax 0161 839 3808
Email archives@gmcro.u-net.com
http://www.u-net.com/~gmcro/
  home.htm

Acting County Archivist:
  Mr Vincent McKernan
Open Mon 1–5; Tues–Fri 9–5;
  second and fourth Sat in month
  9–12, 1–4
Member of the CARN scheme
A fee may be payable (residents of
  Stockport MBC only)
No wheelchair access
Research service
P

Manchester Local Studies Unit Archives (code: 127)
Central Library, St Peter's Square,
  Manchester M2 5PD

Tel 0161 234 1980
Fax 0161 234 1927
Email archives@libraries.manchester.
  gov.uk
http://www.manchester.gov.uk/
  mccdlt/libguide/cenlib/frame.htm

Principal Archivist: Ann Heath
Local Studies Officer: Richard Bond
Open Mon–Thurs 10–4.30
Proof of ID required
Book in advance
Wheelchair access
P M&T D (Manchester)

Medway Archives and Local Studies Centre (code: 1204)
Civic Centre, Strood, Rochester ME2
  4AU

Tel 01634 732714
Fax 01634 297060
Email archives@medway.gov.uk
http://www.medway.gov.uk/

Borough Archivist: Mr Stephen M
Dixon
Open Mon, Thurs, Fri 9–5; Tues 9–6;
first and third Sat in each month
9–1. Closed first two weeks in
November
Member of the CARN scheme
Book in advance
Wheelchair access
P M&T D (Rochester: archdeaconry
of Rochester, and Burham and
Wouldham parish records)

Merseyside Record Office
(code: 1072)
Central Library, William Brown Street,
Liverpool L3 8EW

Tel 0151 233 5817
Fax 0151 207 1342
Email ro@lvpublib.demon.co.uk
http://www.liverpool.gov.uk/

Manager: Mr David Stoker
Open Mon–Thurs 9–7.30; Fri 9–5;
Sat 10–4.
Closed third and fourth weeks in
June
Readers ticket required
Book in advance
Wheelchair access
P

Newham Local Studies Library
(Code: 357)
Stratford Library, Water Lane,
London E15 4NJ

Tel 0181 557 8856
(020 8557 8856)
Fax 0181 503 1525
(020 8503 1525)

Archivist: Richard Durack
Open Mon, Thurs 9.30–8; Tues
9.30–6.30; Fri, Sat 9.30–5.30
Book in advance
Wheelchair access
P

Norfolk Record Office (code: 153)
Gildengate House, Anglia Square,
Upper Green Lane, Norwich NR3
1AX

Tel 01603 761349
Fax 01603 761885
Email norfrec.nro@norfolk.gov.uk
http://www.norfolk.gov.uk/council/
departments/nro/nroindex.htm

County Archivist: Dr John Alban
Open Mon–Fri 9–5; Sat 9–12
Member of the CARN scheme
Book in advance
Wheelchair access
Research service
P M&T D (Norwich. Ely: parish
records of Feltwell and Fincham
deaneries)

Northamptonshire Record Office
(code: 154)
Wootton Hall Park, Northampton
NN4 8BQ

Tel 01604 762129
Fax 01604 767562
Email archivist@
nro.northamptonshire.gov.uk
http://www.nro.northamptonshire.
gov.uk/

County Archivist:
 Miss Rachel Watson
Open Mon–Wed 9–4.45; Thurs
 9–7.45; Fri 9–4.15, two Sat 9–12.15
 each month
Book in advance
Wheelchair access
P M&T D (Peterborough)

Northumberland Record Office
(code: 155)
Melton Park, North Gosforth,
 Newcastle upon Tyne NE3 5QX

Tel 0191 236 2680
Fax 0191 217 0905

Principal Library and Archives
 Officer: Mr Chris Baker
Senior Archivist: Mrs Sue Wood
Open Wed 9.30–1, 2–8; Thurs, Fri
 9.30–1, 2–5
Wheelchair access
Research service
P M&T D (Newcastle)

Nottinghamshire Archives
(code: 157)
County House, Castle Meadow
 Road, Nottingham NG2 1AG

Tel 0115 958 1634/950 4524
Fax 0115 941 3997
http://www.nottscc.gov.uk/

Principal Archivist: Mr AJM
 Henstock
Open Mon, Wed–Fri 9–4.45;
 Tues 9–7.15; Sat 9–12.45
Member of the CARN scheme
Wheelchair access
P M&T D (Southwell)

Oldham Archives Service
(code: 758)
Local Studies Library, 84 Union
 Street, Oldham OL1 1DN

Tel 0161 911 4654
Fax 0161 911 4669
Email archives@oldham.gov.uk
http://www.oldham.gov.uk/archives/

Archivist: Ms M Sienkiewicz
Open Mon, Thurs 10–7; Tues 10–2;
 Wed, Fri, Sat 10–5
Readers ticket required (proof of ID
 in first instance)
Book in advance for microform
 facilities
Wheelchair access

Oxfordshire Archives (code: 160)
County Hall, New Road, Oxford OX1
 1ND

Tel 01865 815203
Fax 01865 815429
Email archives.occdla@dial.
 pipex.com

County Archivist: Mr Carl Boardman
Open Mon–Thurs 9–5. Closed for
 stocktaking end of Jan/beginning of
 Feb
Member of the CARN scheme
Book in advance
Wheelchair access
Research service
P M&T D (Oxford)

Peterborough Central Library
(code: 1189)
Broadway, Peterborough PE1 1RX

Tel 01733 348343
Fax 01733 555277

Local Studies Librarian: Mr Richard
  Hillier
Open by appointment
Wheelchair access

**Plymouth and West Devon Area
Record Office (code: 28)**
Unit 3, Clare Place, Coxside,
  Plymouth PL4 OJW

Tel 01752 305940
Fax 01752 223939
Email pwdro@plymouth.gov.uk

City Archivist: Mr Paul Brough
Open Tues–Thurs 9.30–5;
  Fri 9.30–4.30
Member of the CARN scheme
Book in advance
A fee may be payable
Special arrangements for wheelchairs
P M&T D (Exeter: Plymouth
  archdeaconry)

**Portsmouth City Museums and
Records Service (code: 42)**
Museum Road, Portsmouth PO1 2LJ

Tel 01705 827261
  (023 9282 7261)
Fax 01705 875276
  (023 9287 5276)
Email portmus@compuserve.com
http://ourworld.compuserve.com/
  homepages/portmus/

Museums and Records Officer:
  Mrs SE Quail
Open Mon–Fri 10–5
Member of the CARN scheme
Wheelchair access
Research service
P M&T D (Portsmouth: parish
  records of Portsmouth, Havant,
  Fareham and Gosport deaneries)

**Redbridge Local Studies and
Archives (code: 90)**
Local History Room, Clements Road,
  Ilford IG1 1EA

Tel 0181 478 9421
  (020 8478 9421)
Fax 0181 553 3299
  (020 8553 3299)

Archivist: Mr Tudor Allen
Open Mon–Fri 9.30–8; Sat 9.30–4
Wheelchair access

**Rochdale Libraries, Local Studies
Department (code: 128)**
Arts and Heritage Centre, Esplanade,
  Rochdale OL16 1AQ

Tel 01706 647474

Local Studies Officer:
  Mrs PA Godman
Open Tues, Wed, Fri 10–1, 2–5.30;
  Thurs 10–1, 2–7.30; Sat 9.30–1, 2–4
Wheelchair access

**Rotherham Metropolitan Borough
Archives and Local Studies Section
(code: 198)**
Brian O'Malley Central Library,
  Walker Place, Rotherham S65 1JH

Tel 01709 823616/382121 ext 3616
Fax 01709 823650
Email archives@rotherham.gov.uk
http://www.rotherham.gov.uk/

Manager: Mr AP Munford
Open Tues, Wed, Fri 10–5;
  Thurs 1–7; Sat 9.30–1, 2–4
Book in advance for microform
  facilities
Wheelchair access
Research service
P M&T

St Helens Local History and Archives Library (code: 139)
Central Library, Gamble Institute, Victoria Square, St Helens WA10 1DY

Tel 01744 456952
Fax 01744 20836

Local History Librarian and Archivist: Mrs VL Hainsworth
Open Mon, Wed 9.30–8; Tues, Thurs, Fri 9.30–5; Sat 9.30–4
Book in advance
Wheelchair access

Salford Archives Centre (code: 129)
658–662 Liverpool Road, Irlam, Manchester M44 5AD

Tel 0161 775 5643

City Archivist: Mr AN Cross
Open Mon–Fri 9–4.30
Readers ticket required (proof of ID in first instance)
Book in advance
No wheelchair access
P

Sandwell Community History and Archives Service (code: 146)
Smethwick Library, High Street, Smethwick, Warley B66 1AB

Tel 0121 558 2561
Fax 0121 555 6064
http://www.earl.org.uk/partners/ sandwell/

Borough Archivist: Miss CM Harrington
Open Mon 9.30–7; Tues, Wed, Fri 9.30–6; Sat 9.30–4
Book in advance
Wheelchair access
P D (Birmingham: Warley deanery)

Shakespeare Birthplace Trust Records Office (code: 188)
Shakespeare Centre, Stratford-upon-Avon CV37 6QW

Tel 01789 204016/201816
Fax 01789 296083
Email records@shakespeare.org.uk
http://www.shakespeare.org.uk/

Senior Archivist: Dr R Bearman
Open Mon–Fri 9.30–1, 2–5; Sat 9.30–12.30
Wheelchair access
P M&T D (Coventry: parish records of Stratford-upon-Avon and Shottery)

Sheffield Archives (code: 199)
52 Shoreham Street, Sheffield S1 4SP

Tel 0114 273 4756
Fax 0114 203 9398
Email sheffieldarchives @dial.pipex.com

Group Manager, Archives and Local Studies: Mrs Margaret Turner
Open Mon–Thurs 9.30–5.30; Sat 9–1, 2–4.30
Readers ticket required
Book in advance
Wheelchair access
Research service
P M&T D (Sheffield)

Shropshire Records and Research Centre (code: 166)
Castle Gates, Shrewsbury SY1 2AQ

Tel 01743 255350
Fax 01743 255355
Email m.mckenzie @shropshire-cc.gov.uk
http://www.shropshire-cc.gov.uk/

Head of Records and Research:
Miss Mary McKenzie
Open Tues 10–9; Wed–Fri 10–5;
Sat 10–4
Readers ticket required
Book in advance for microform
facilities
Wheelchair access
Research service
HMC P D (Hereford: parish records
of Ludlow archdeaconry. Lichfield:
parish records of Salop
archdeaconry)

**Somerset Archive and Record
Service (code: 168)**
Obridge Road, Taunton TA2 7PU

Tel 01823 278805/337600
(appointments)
Fax 01823 325402
Email Somerset_Archives@
compuserve.com
http://www.somerset.gov.uk/
archives/

County Archivist: Mr Adam Green
Open Mon 2–4.50; Tues–Thurs
9–4.50; Fri 9–4.20; alternate Sat
9.15–12.15. Closed first full week of
February and the preceding week
Member of CARN scheme
Book in advance
Wheelchair access
Research service
HMC P D (Bath and Wells)

**Southampton Archives Services
(code: 43)**
Civic Centre, Southampton SO14 7LY

Tel 01703 832251
(023 8083 2251
Fax 01703 832156
(023 8083 2156)
Email city.archives@southampton.
gov.uk
http://www.southampton.gov.uk/

Archives Services Manager:
Mrs SL Woolgar
Open Tues–Fri 9.30–4.30; one
evening a month to 9 by
appointment
Wheelchair access
Research service
P M&T D (Winchester: Southampton
parish records)

**Southwark Local Studies Library
(code: 91)**
211 Borough High Street, London
SE1 1JA

Tel 0171 403 3507
(020 7403 3507)
Fax 0171 403 8633
(020 7403 8633)

Local Studies Librarian:
Mr Leonard Reilly
Open Mon, Thurs 9.30–8; Tues,
Fri 9.30–5; Sat 9.30–1
Book in advance
Wheelchair access

**Staffordshire and Stoke-on-Trent
Archive Service, Staffordshire
Record Office (code: 169)**
Eastgate Street, Stafford ST16 2LZ

Tel 01785 278379
Fax 01785 278384
Minicom 01785 278376
Email staffordshire.record.office@
staffordshire.gov.uk
http://www.staffordshire.gov.uk/
archives/

Head of Archive Services:
Mrs Thea Randall
Principal Archivist: Mr Mark
Dorrington
Open Mon–Thurs 9–5; Fri 9.30–4.30;
Sat 9–12.30
Readers ticket required (proof of ID
in first instance)
Book in advance
Wheelchair access
Research service
HMC P D (Lichfield: parish records of
Stafford archdeaconry)

**Staffordshire and Stoke-on-Trent
Archive Service, Burton upon Trent
Archives (code: 494)**
Burton upon Trent Public Library,
Riverside, High Street, Burton upon
Trent, Staffordshire DE14 1AH

Tel 01283 239556
Fax 01283 239571
Email burton.library@staffordshire.
gov.uk
http://www.staffordshire.gov.uk/
archives/burton.htm

Head of Archive Services:
Mrs Thea Randall
Archivist in charge:
Mr Martin Sanders
Open Mon, Tues, Thurs, Fri 9.15–12,
2–6; Wed 9.15–1
Readers ticket required (proof of ID
in first instance)
Book in advance
Wheelchair access

**Staffordshire and Stoke-on-Trent
Archive Service, Lichfield Record
Office (code: 171)**
Lichfield Library, The Friary, Lichfield
WS13 6QG

Tel 01543 510720
Fax 01543 510715
Email lichfield.record.office@
staffordshire.gov.uk
http://www.staffordshire.gov.uk/
archives/lich.htm

Head of Archive Services:
Mrs Thea Randall
Archivist in charge:
Mr Martin Sanders
Open Mon–Fri 9.30–5; second Sat in
month 9.30–12.30 by appointment
Readers ticket required (proof of ID
in first instance)
Book in advance
Wheelchair access
Research service
P M&T D (Lichfield)

**Staffordshire and Stoke-on-Trent
Archive Service, Stoke-on-Trent
City Archives (code: 1857)**
Hanley Library, Bethesda Street,
Stoke-on-Trent ST1 3RS

Tel 01782 238420
Fax 01782 238499
Email stoke.archives@stoke.gov.uk
http://www.staffordshire.gov.uk/
archives/contact2.htm

Head of Archive Services:
Mrs Thea Randall
Senior Archivist: Mr Chris Latimer
Open Wed 9.30–7; Thurs, Fri 9.30–5;
Sat 9.30–1
Readers ticket required (proof of ID
in first instance)
Book in advance
Wheelchair access
Research service

Staffordshire and Stoke-on-Trent Archive Service, William Salt Library (code: 170)
Eastgate Street, Stafford ST16 2LZ

Tel 01785 278372
Fax 01785 278414
Email
william.salt@staffordshire.gov.uk
http://www.staffordshire.gov.uk/
archives/salt.htm

Librarian: Mrs Thea Randall
Open Tues–Thurs 9–1, 2–5; Fri 9–1,
2–4.30; first Sat in month 9–1
Readers ticket required (proof of ID
in first instance)
Wheelchair access
Research service
M&T

N.B. The Library is administered by
the Archive Service but does not
officially form part of it.

**Stockport Archive Service
(code: 130)**
Heritage Library, Wellington Road
South, Stockport SK1 3RS

Tel 0161 474 4530
Fax 0161 474 7750
Email stockport.cenlibrary@
dial.pipex.com

Archivist: Mrs MJ Myerscough
Open Mon, Tues, Fri 10–8; Wed,
Thurs 10–5; Sat 9–4
Book in advance
Wheelchair access
P

**Suffolk Record Office, Bury St
Edmunds Branch (code: 174)**
77 Raingate Street, Bury St Edmunds
IP33 2AR

Tel 01284 352352
Fax 01284 352355
Email gwyn.thomas@libher.
suffolkcc.gov.uk
http://www.suffolkcc.gov.uk/
libraries_and_heritage/sro/

Senior Area Archivist:
Mr Gwyn Thomas
Open Mon–Sat 9–5
Member of the CARN scheme
Wheelchair access
Research service
P M&T D (St Edmundsbury and
Ipswich: Sudbury archdeaconry
and Hadleigh deanery)

**Suffolk Record Office, Ipswich
Branch (code: 173)**
Gatacre Road, Ipswich IP1 2LQ

Tel 01473 584541
Fax 01473 584533
Email gwyn.thomas@libher.
suffolkcc.gov.uk
http://www.suffolkcc.gov.uk/
libraries_and_heritage/sro/

Senior Area Archivist:
Mr Gwyn Thomas
Open Mon–Sat 9–5
Member of CARN scheme
Book in advance
Wheelchair access
Research service
P M&T D (St Edmundsbury and
Ipswich: Ipswich and Suffolk
archdeaconries)

**Suffolk Record Office, Lowestoft
Branch (code: 175)**
Central Library, Clapham Road,
Lowestoft NR32 1DR

Tel 01502 405357
Fax 01502 405350
Email lowestoft.ro@
  libher.suffolkcc.gov.uk
http://www.suffolkcc.gov.uk/
  libraries_and_heritage/sro/

Area Archivist: Miss Kate Chantry
Open Mon, Wed–Fri 9.15–5.30; Tues
  9.15–6; Sat 9.15–5
Member of CARN scheme
Book in advance for microform
  facilities
Wheelchair access
Research service
P M&T D (St Edmundsbury and
  Ipswich: NE Suffolk parish records)

Surrey History Centre (code: 176)
130 Goldsworth Road, Woking GU21
  1ND

Tel 01483 594594
Fax 01483 594595
Email shs@surreycc.gov.uk
http://shs.surreycc.gov.uk/

County Archivist: Dr DB Robinson
Open Tues, Wed, Fri 9.30–5;
  Thurs 9.30–7.30; Sat 9.30–4
Closed Bank Holiday weekends
  (incl Sat)
Member of the CARN scheme
Wheelchair access
Research service
P M&T D (Southwark: parish
  records. Guildford: parish records of
  Emly and Epsom deaneries)

N.B. includes records from both
  Surrey Record Office and Guildford
  Muniment Room.

**East Sussex Record Office
(code: 179)**
The Maltings, Castle Precincts,
  Lewes BN7 1YT
Tel 01273 482349
Fax 01273 482341
http://www.eastsussexcc.gov.uk/

County Archivist: Mr Roger Davey
Open Mon, Tues, Thurs 8.45–4.45;
  Wed 9.30–4.45; Fri 8.45–4.15;
  second Sat of month 9–1, 2–4.45
Member of the CARN scheme
Wheelchair access
Research service
P D (Chichester: East Sussex parish
  records)

**West Sussex Record Office
(code: 182)**
Sherburne House, 3 Orchard Street,
  Chichester
Correspondence address: County
  Hall, Chichester PO19 1RN

Tel 01243 533911
Fax 01243 533959
Email records.office@
  westsussex.gov.uk
http://www.westsussex.gov.uk/cs/ro/

County Archivist: Mr Richard Childs
Open Mon–Fri 9.15–4.45; Sat
  9.15–12.30, 1.30–4.30. Closed one
  week in early December
Member of the CARN scheme
Wheelchair access
Research service
P M&T D (Chichester)

**Sutton Heritage Services, Archive
Section (code: 362)**
Archive and Local Studies
  Searchroom, Central Library, St
  Nicholas Way, Sutton SM1 1EA

Tel 0181 770 4747/4745
(020 8770 4747/4745)
Fax 0181 770 4777
(020 8770 4777)
Email sutton.heritage@dial.pipex.com
http://www.sutton.gov.uk/

Archivist: Ms Kathleen Shawcross
Open Tues, Fri 9.30–12; Wed, Thurs
2–7.30; first and third Sat in month
9.30–1, 2–4.45; first and third Sun in
month 2–5
Sutton Library ticket or proof of ID
required
Book in advance
Wheelchair access
Research service
P M&T

**Tameside Archive Service
(code: 131)**
Tameside Local Studies Library,
Astley Cheetham Public Library,
Trinity Street, Stalybridge SK15
2BN

Tel 0161 338 2708/3831
Fax 0161 303 8289
Email tamelocal@dial.pipex.com
http://dspace.dial.pipex.com/town/
street/xlx81/index.htm

Archivist: Miss Helen Mackie
Open Mon–Wed, Fri 9–7.30; Sat 9–4
Book in advance for microform
facilities
No wheelchair access
P

Teesside Archives (code: 20)
Exchange House, 6 Marton Road,
Middlesbrough TS1 1DB

Tel 01642 248321
Fax 01642 248391

County Archivist: Mr DH Tyrell
Open Mon, Wed, Thurs 9–5;
Tues 9–9; Fri 9–4.30
Member of the CARN scheme
Book in advance
Wheelchair access
P D (York: Cleveland parish records)

**Tower Hamlets Local History
Library and Archives (code: 92)**
Bancroft Library, 277 Bancroft Road,
London E1 4DQ

Tel 0181 980 4366 ext 129
(020 8980 4366 ext 129)
Fax 0181 983 4510
(020 8983 4510)

Archivist: Mr Malcolm Barr-Hamilton
Open Mon, Tues, Thurs 9–8; Fri 9–6;
Sat 9–5
Book in advance for microform
facilities

**Trafford Local Studies Centre
(code: 742)**
Sale Library, Tatton Road, Sale M33
1YH

Tel 0161 912 3013
Fax 0161 912 3019
Email
trafford.local.studies@free4all.co.uk

Local Studies Librarian:
Ms Pat Southam
Open Mon, Thurs 10–7.30; Tues,
Fri 10–5; Sat 10–4
Book in advance
Wheelchair access
Research service

**Tyne and Wear Archives Service
(code: 183)**
Blandford House, Blandford Square,
Newcastle upon Tyne NE1 4JA

Tel 0191 232 6789
Fax 0191 230 2614
Email twas@dial.pipex.com
http://ris.niaa.org.uk/archives/

Chief Archivist: Ms EA Rees
Open Mon, Wed–Fri 9–5.15;
 Tues 9–8.30
Proof of ID required
Book in advance for microform
 facilities
Wheelchair access
Research service
P M&T

**Walsall Archives Service
(code: 148)**
Local History Centre, Essex Street,
 Walsall WS2 7AS

Tel 01922 721305/6
Fax 01922 634954
http://www.earl.org.uk/partners/
 walsall/

Archivist/Local Studies Officer:
 Ms Ruth Vyse
Open Tues, Thurs 9.30–5.30; Wed
 9.30–7; Fri 9.30–5; Sat 9.30–1
Book in advance
Wheelchair access
P M&T

**Waltham Forest Archives and Local
Studies Library (code: 93)**
Vestry House Museum, Vestry Road,
 Walthamstow, London E17 9NH

Tel 0181 509 1917
 (020 8509 1917)
Fax 0181 509 9539
 (020 8509 9539)
http://www.lbwf.gov.uk/

Archivist: Ms Josephine Parker
Open Tues, Wed, Fri 10–1, 2–5.15;
 Sat 10–1, 2–4.45. Closed for two
 weeks, usually in December.
Book in advance
Special arrangements for wheelchairs
M&T D (Chelmsford: parish records
 of Waltham Forest deanery)

**Wandsworth Local History
Collection (code: 347)**
Battersea Library, 265 Lavender Hill,
 London SW11 1JB

Tel 0181 871 7753
 (020 8871 7753)
Fax 0171 978 4376
 (020 7978 4376)
http://www.wandsworth.gov.uk/

Archivist: post vacant
Open Tues, Wed 10–1, 2–8; Fri 10–1,
 2–5; Sat 9–1
Book in advance

Warrington Library (code: 19)
Museum Street, Warrington WA1
 1JB

Tel 01925 442890
Fax 01925 411395
Email library@warrington.gov.uk
http://www.warrington.gov.uk/

Libraries and Information Services
 Manager: Ms Janet Hill
Open Mon, Tues, Fri 9.30–7; Wed
 9.30–5; Thurs 9.30–1; Sat 9–1
Book in advance
Wheelchair access
Research service (via Cheshire
 Record Office)
M&T

Warwickshire County Record Office (code: 187)
Priory Park, Cape Road, Warwick
   CV34 4JS

Tel 01926 412735
Fax 01926 412509
Email warwickshire.archives@
   dial.pipex.com
http://www.warwickshire.gov.uk/
   general/rcindex.htm

County Archivist:
   Ms Caroline Sampson
Open Tues–Thurs 9–5.30; Fri 9–5;
   Sat 9–12.30
Readers ticket required
Wheelchair access
Research service
P M&T D (Coventry. Birmingham:
   parish records)

City of Westminster Archives Centre (code: 94)
10 St Ann's Street, London SW1P
   2DE

Tel 0171 641 5180
   (020 7641 5180)
Fax 0171 641 5179
   (020 7641 5179)
http://www.westminster.gov.uk/el/
   libarch/index.html

City Archivist: Mr Jerome Farrell
Open Mon, Tues, Thurs, Fri 9.30–7;
   Wed 9.30–9; Sat 9.30–5
Wheelchair access
P M&T D (London: Westminster
   parish records)

Wigan Archives Service (code: 132)
Town Hall, Leigh WN7 2DY

Tel 01942 404430
Fax 01942 404425
Email heritage@wiganmbc.gov.uk
http://www.wiganmbc.gov.uk/

Heritage Service Manager:
   Mr AD Gillies
Archivist: Mr NP Webb
Open Mon, Tues, Thurs, Fri 10–1,
   2–4.30
Book in advance
Wheelchair access
P M&T D (Liverpool: parish records
   of Wigan and Winwick deaneries)

Wiltshire and Swindon Record Office (code: 190)
County Hall, Trowbridge BA14 8BS

Tel 01225 713136
Fax 01225 713993

Principal Archivist: Mr JN d'Arcy
Open Mon, Tues, Thurs, Fri 9.15–5;
   Wed 9.15–7.45. Closed last fortnight
   in January
Member of the CARN scheme
Wheelchair access
P M&T D (Salisbury. Bristol: parish
   records of Swindon archdeaconry)

Wirral Archives Service (code: 140)
Birkenhead Reference Library,
   Borough Road, Birkenhead CH41
   2XB

Tel 0151 652 6106
Fax 0151 653 7320

Archivist: post vacant
Open Mon, Tues, Thurs 10–8;
   Fri 10–5; Sat 10–1, 2–5
Proof of ID required
Book in advance
Special arrangements for wheelchairs
P

Wolverhampton Archives and Local Studies (code: 149)
42–50 Snow Hill, Wolverhampton
WV2 4AG

Tel 01902 552480
Fax 01902 552481
Email wolvarch.and.ls@
dial.pipex.com
http://www.wolverhampton.gov.uk/
library/archives.htm

Borough Archivist: Mr Paul Sillitoe
Open Mon, Tues, Fri 10–5; Wed
10–7; first and third Sat in month
10–5. Closed one week in November
Member of the CARN scheme
Book in advance for microform
facilities
Wheelchair access
Research service
P

Worcestershire Record Office, Headquarters Branch (code: 45)
County Hall, Spetchley Road,
Worcester WR5 2NP

Tel 01905 766351
Fax 01905 766363
Email
RecordOffice@worcestershire.gov.uk
http://www.worcestershire.gov.uk/

County Archivist: Mr AM Wherry
Open Mon 10–4.45; Tues–Thurs
9.15–4.45; Fri 9.15–4. Closed second
and third weeks of November
Member of CARN scheme
Book in advance
Wheelchair access
Research service
P M&T D (Worcester)

Worcestershire Record Office, City Centre Branch (code: 781)
St Helen's Church, Fish Street,
Worcester WR1 2HN

Tel 01905 765922
Fax 01905 765925
Email corr@worcestershire.gov.uk
http://www.worcestershire.gov.uk/

Head of Repository: Miss Claire Orr
Open Mon 10–4.45; Tues–Thurs
9.15–4.45; Fri 9.15–4. Closed second
and third weeks of November
Member of the CARN scheme
Book in advance for microform
facilities
Wheelchair access
Research service
M&T D (Worcester)

York City Archives Department (code: 192)
Art Gallery Building, Exhibition
Square, York Y01 7EW

Tel 01904 551878/9
Fax 01904 551877

City Archivist: Mrs RJ Freedman
Open Mon–Fri 9–1, 2–5
Wheelchair access
P M&T

North Yorkshire County Record Office (code: 191)
Malpas Road, Northallerton
Correspondence address: County
Hall, Northallerton DL7 8AF

Tel 01609 777585
Fax 01609 777078

County Archivist: Mr MY Ashcroft
Open Mon, Tues, Thurs 9–4.45; Wed
  9–8.45; Fri 9–4.15
Book in advance
Wheelchair access
Research service
P D (Bradford, Ripon, York: parish
  records)

**East Riding of Yorkshire Archive
Office (code: 47)**
County Hall, Beverley HU17 9BA

Tel 01482 885007
Fax 01482 885463
Email Mike.Rogers@east-riding-of-
yorkshire.gov.uk

Archivist: Mr Ian Mason
Open Mon, Wed, Thurs 9–1, 2–4.45;
  Tues 9–1, 2–8; Fri 9–1, 2–4. Closed
  last week in January
Book in advance
Wheelchair access
Research service
P M&T D (York: parish records of the
  East Riding archdeaconry)

N.B. Searchoom will be temporarily
  relocated in 1999. Searchers should
  check availability of records in
  advance.

**West Yorkshire Archive Service,
Wakefield Headquarters (code: 201)**
Registry of Deeds, Newstead Road,
  Wakefield WF1 2DE

Tel 01924 305980
Fax 01924 305983
Email enquiries@wakefieldarchives.
  freeserve.co.uk
http://www.archives.wyjs.org.uk/

County Archivist:
  Mrs Sylvia Thomas
Area Manager: Mr Keith Sweetmore
Principal District Archivist:
  Mrs Ruth Harris
Open Mon 9.30–1, 2–8; Tues, Wed
  9.30–1, 2–5. Closed one week in
  February
Book in advance
No wheelchair access
Research service
P M&T D (Wakefield)

**West Yorkshire Archive Service,
Bradford (code: 202)**
15 Canal Road, Bradford BD1 4AT

Tel 01274 731931
Fax 01274 734013
Email enquiries@bradfordarchives.
  freeserve.co.uk
http://www.archives.wyjs.org.uk/

County Archivist:
  Mrs Sylvia Thomas
Principal District Archivist:
  Mr Andrew George
Open Mon–Thurs 9.30–1, 2–5;
  alternate Thurs to 8. Closed one
  week in February
Book in advance
No wheelchair access
Research service
P D (Bradford)

**West Yorkshire Archive Service,
Calderdale (code: 203)**
Central Library, Northgate House,
  Northgate, Halifax HX1 1UN

Tel 01422 392636
Fax 01422 341083
Email enq@wyashq.demon.co.uk
http://www.archives.wyjs.org.uk/

County Archivist:
  Mrs Sylvia Thomas
Principal District Archivist:
  Miss Pat Sewell
Open Mon, Tues, Thurs, Fri 10–5.30.
  Open evenings to 7 and Sat 10–5
  for microform only. Closed first
  week in February and first week in
  November
Book in advance
Wheelchair access
Research service
P M&T D (Bradford: Shelf St Michael
  parish records)

**West Yorkshire Archive Service,
Kirklees (code: 204)**
Central Library, Princess Alexandra
  Walk, Huddersfield HD1 2SU

Tel 01484 221966
Fax 01484 518361
Email enq@wyashq.demon.co.uk
http://www.archives.wyjs.org.uk/

County Archivist:
  Mrs Sylvia Thomas
Principal District Archivist:
  Miss Janet Burhouse
Open Mon, Thurs 10–5, Tues 10–8;
  Fri 10–1. Closed one week in
  February
Book in advance
Wheelchair access
Research service
P M&T

**West Yorkshire Archive Service,
Leeds (code: 205)**
Chapeltown Road, Sheepscar, Leeds
  LS7 3AP

Tel 0113 214 5814
Fax 0113 214 5815
Email enq@wyashq.demon.co.uk
http://www.archives.wyjs.org.uk/

County Archivist:
  Mrs Sylvia Thomas
Principal District Archivist:
  Mr WJ Connor
Open Tues–Fri 9.30–5. Closed one
  week in February
Book in advance
No wheelchair access
Research service
P M&T D (Ripon: Bradford parish
  records)

**West Yorkshire Archive Service,
Yorkshire Archaeological Society
(code: 207)**
Claremont, 23 Clarendon Road, Leeds
  LS2 9NZ

Tel 0113 245 6362
Fax 0113 244 1979
Email enq@wyashq.demon.co.uk
http://www.archives.wyjs.org.uk/

County Archivist:
  Mrs Sylvia Thomas
Archivist in charge: Mr WJ Connor
YAS Senior Librarian and Archivist:
  Mr RL Frost
Open Tues, Wed 2–8.30; Thurs–Sat
  9.30–5
Book in advance
Wheelchair access
Research service
M&T

WALES

Offices appear in alphabetical order
of name in English (as given on the
Archive Council Wales website)

**Anglesey County Record Office
(code: 221)**
Shire Hall, Glanhwfa Road, Llangefni
  LL77 7TW

Tel 01248 752080
http://www.anglesey.gov.uk/

Archivist: Ms Anne Venables
Open Mon–Fri 9–1, 2–5. Closed first
full week in November
Member of the CARN scheme
Book in advance for microform
facilities
Special arrangements for wheelchairs
Research service
P M&T D (Bangor: Anglesey parish
records)

Carmarthenshire Record Office (code: 211)
County Hall, Carmarthen SA31 1JP

Tel 01267 224184
Fax 01267 224104
Email archives@carmarthenshire.
gov.uk
http://www.llgc.org.uk/cac/
cac0028.htm

County Archivist: Mr John Davies
Open Mon–Thurs 9–4.45; Fri 9–4.15
Book in advance
Wheelchair access
Research service
P M&T D (St Davids: parish records)

Ceredigion Archives (code: 212)
County Office, Marine Terrace,
Aberystwyth SY23 2DE

Tel 01970 633697/8
Fax 01970 633663
Email archives@ceredigion.gov.uk
http://www.llgc.org.uk/cac/
cac0009.htm

Archivist: Miss Helen Palmer
Open Mon–Fri 10–1, 2–4
Member of the CARN scheme
Wheelchair access
P M&T D (St Davids: parish records)

Denbighshire Record Office (code: 209)
46 Clwyd Street, Ruthin LL15 1HP

Tel 01824 708250
Fax 01824 708258
Email archives@denbighshire.gov.uk
http://www.denbighshire.gov.uk/

County Archivist: Mr RK Matthias
Open Mon–Thurs 9–4.45; Fri 9–4.15
Member of the CARN scheme
Book in advance for microform
facilities
Wheelchair access
Research service
P M&T D (St Asaph: parish records)

N.B. Remit covers Denbighshire as a
new local authority area. Public,
official and deposited records for
those parts of the historic county of
Denbighshire outside this area are
collected only where these are
additions to existing series.

Flintshire Record Office (code: 208)
The Old Rectory, Hawarden,
Flintshire CH5 3NR

Tel 01244 532364
Fax 01244 538344
Email archives@flintshire.gov.uk
http://www.llgc.org.uk/cac/
cac0032.htm

County Archivist: Mr Rowland
Williams
Open Mon–Thurs 9–4.45; Fri 9–4.15
Member of the CARN scheme
Book in advance
Wheelchair access
P M&T D (St Asaph: parish records)

N.B. Remit covers Flintshire as a new local authority area. Public, official and deposited records for those parts of the historic county of Flintshire outside this area are collected only where these are additions to existing series.

Glamorgan Record Office (code: 214)

Glamorgan Building, King Edward VII Avenue, Cathays Park, Cardiff CF1 3NE

Tel 01222 780282
(029 2078 0282)
Fax 01222 780284
(029 2078 0284)
http://www.llgc.org.uk/cac/
  cac0026.htm

Glamorgan Archivist: Miss Susan Edwards
Open Tues–Thurs 9.30–1, 2–5; Fri 9.30–1, 2–4.30; Wed open to 7 by appointment
Book in advance for microform facilities
A fee may be payable for microform facilities
Wheelchair access
Research service
P M&T D (Llandaff: parish records)

West Glamorgan Archive Service (code: 216)

County Hall, Oystermouth Road, Swansea SA1 3SN

Tel 01792 636589
Fax 01792 637130
Email susan.beckley
  @swansea.gov.uk
http://www.swansea.gov.uk/culture/
  laarindex.htm

County Archivist: Miss SG Beckley
Open Mon–Thurs 9–5; Mon 5.30–7.30 by arrangement
Book in advance for microform facilities
Wheelchair access
Research service
P M&T D (Swansea and Brecon: parish records)

Gwent Record Office (code: 218)

County Hall, Cwmbran NP44 2XH

Tel 01633 644886
Fax 01633 648382
Email 113057.2173@compuserve.com
http://www.llgc.org.uk/cac/
  cac0004.htm

County Archivist: Mr David Rimmer
Open Tues–Thurs 9.30–5; Fri 9.30–4
Member of the CARN scheme
Book in advance
Wheelchair access
P M&T D (Swansea and Brecon, Monmouth: parish records)

Gwynedd Archives and Museums Service, Caernarfon Record Office (code: 219)

Victoria Dock, Caernarfon
Correspondence address: Education and Culture Department, County Offices, Shirehall Street, Caernarfon LL55 1SH

Tel 01286 679095/679088
  (Principal Archivist)
Fax 01286 679637
Email AnnRhydderch
  @gwynedd.gov.uk
http://www.llgc.org.uk/cac/
  cac0053.htm

Principal Archivist and Museums
Officer: Ann Rhydderch
Open Tues–Fri 9.30–12.30, 1.30–5;
Wed to 7. Closed second full week
in October
Member of the CARN scheme
Wheelchair access
Research service
P M&T D (Bangor, St Asaph: parish
records)

**Gwynedd Archives and Museums
Service, Merioneth Archives
(Archifdy Meirion) (code: 220)**
Cae Penarlag, Dolgellau LL40 2YB

Tel 01341 424444
Fax 01341 424505
http://www.llgc.org.uk/cac/
cac0030.htm

Archivist: Mr E W Thomas
Open Mon, Wed–Fri 9–1, 2–5. Closed
first full week in November
Member of the CARN scheme
Wheelchair access
Research service
P M&T D (Bangor, St Asaph: parish
records)

**Pembrokeshire Record Office
(code: 213)**
The Castle, Haverfordwest SA61 2EF

Tel 01437 763707
http://www.llgc.org.uk/cac/
cac0002.htm

County Archivist: Mr John Owen
Open Mon–Thurs 9–4.45; Fri 9–4.15;
first Sat in month 9.30–12.30 (except
bank holiday weekends)
Wheelchair access
Research service
P M&T D (St Davids parish records)

**Powys County Archives Office
(code: 223)**
County Hall, Llandrindod Wells LD1
5LG

Tel 01597 826088
Fax 01597 827162
Email archives@powys.gov.uk
http://archives.powys.gov.uk/

County Archivist: Mr Gordon Reid
Open Tues–Thurs 10–12.30, 1.30–5;
Fri 9–12.30, 1.30–4
Member of the CARN scheme
Book in advance
Wheelchair access
P D (Bangor, Swansea and Brecon,
St Asaph: parish records)

SCOTLAND

Aberdeen City Archives (code: 230)
The Town House, Broad Street,
Aberdeen AB10 1AQ

Tel 01224 522513
Fax 01224 522491
Email ARCHIVES@LEGAL.
aberdeen.net.uk

City Archivist: Miss Judith Cripps
Open Wed–Fri 9.30–4.30
Book in advance
Special arrangements for wheelchairs
Research service
P (Scotland)

**Aberdeen City Archives, Old
Aberdeen House Branch (code : 228)**
Old Aberdeen House, Dunbar Street,
Aberdeen AB24 1LU

Tel 01224 481775
Fax 01224 495830
Email ARCHIVES@LEGAL.
aberdeen.net.uk

City Archivist: Miss Judith Cripps
Open : Mon–Wed 9.30–1 2–4.30.
  Closed first two weeks in December
Book in advance
Wheelchair access
Research service

N.B. The branch administers the
records of the former Grampian
Regional Archives and houses most
post 1996 accessions to Aberdeen
City Archives.

Angus Archives (code: 618)
Montrose Library, 214 High Street,
  Montrose DD10 8PH

Tel 01674 671415
Fax 01674 671810
Email archives@angus.gov.uk
http://www.angus.gov.uk/history/

Local Studies Librarian:
  Mrs Fiona Scharlau
Open M–F 9.30–5
Proof of ID required
Book in advance
No wheelchair access
Research service

Argyll and Bute Council Archives (code: 245)
Manse Brae, Lochgilphead PA31
  8QU

Tel 01546 604120
Fax 01546 606897

Archivist: Mr Murdo MacDonald
Open Tues–Fri 10–1, 2–4.30
Book in advance
No wheelchair access

Ayrshire Archives (code: 244)
Ayrshire Archives Centre, Craigie
  Estate, Ayr KA8 0SS

Tel 01292 287584
Fax 01292 284918
Email kwilbraham@south-ayrshire.
  gov.uk
http://www.south-ayrshire.gov.uk/

Archivist in charge:
  Mr Kevin Wilbraham
Open Tue–Thurs 10–4
Proof of ID required
Book in advance
Wheelchair access
Research service
P (Scotland)

Dumfries and Galloway Archives (code: 226)
Archive Centre, 33 Burns Street,
  Dumfries DG1 2PS

Tel 01387 269254
Fax 01387 264126

Archivist: Miss MM Stewart
Open Tues, Wed, Fri 11–1, 2–5;
  Thurs 6–9 (evening)
Book in advance
Wheelchair access
Research service
P (Scotland)

Dumfries and Galloway Libraries (code: 225)
Ewart Library, Catherine Street,
  Dumfries DG1 1JB

Tel 01387 253820
Fax 01387 260294
Email libs&i@dumgal.gov.uk
http://146.176.15.249:80/ISC453/

Reference and Local Studies
  Librarian: Ms Ruth Airley
Open Mon–Wed, Fri 10–7.30; Thurs,
  Sat 10–5
Book in advance
Wheelchair access
Research service
P (Scotland)

N.B. Forms part of the archives
service. All general enquiries should
be addressed in the first instance to
Miss MM Stewart at the Archive
Centre.

Dundee City Archives (code: 251)
1 Shore Terrace, Dundee
Correspondence address:
  Department of Support Services, 21
  City Square, Dundee DD1 3BY

Tel 01382 434494
Fax 01382 434666
Email iain.flett@dundeecity.gov.uk
http://www.dundeecity.gov.uk/

City Archivist: Mr IEF Flett
Open Mon–Fri 9.15–1, 2–4.45
Proof of ID required
Book in advance
Wheelchair access
P (Scotland)

N.B. Relevant local collections have
been transferred to Angus Archives
and to Perth and Kinross Council
Archive. Holds the core records of
the former Tayside Regional Council.

Edinburgh City Archives (code: 236)
Department of Corporate Services,
  City of Edinburgh Council, City
  Chambers, High Street, Edinburgh
  EH1 1YJ

Tel 0131 529 4616
Fax 0131 529 4957

City Archivist: Mr Richard Hunter
Open Mon–Thurs 9–4.30
Wheelchair access

**Falkirk Museums History Research
Centre (code: 558)**
Callendar House, Callendar Park,
  Falkirk FK1 1YR

Tel 01324 503770
Fax 01324 503711
Email callendarhouse
  @falkirkmuseums.demon.co.uk
http://www.falkirkmuseums.
  demon.co.uk

Archivist: Ms Elspeth Reid
Open Mon–Fri 10–12.30, 1.30–5
Book in advance
Wheelchair access
Research service

Glasgow City Archives (code: 243)
The Mitchell Library, 201 North
  Street, Glasgow G3 7DN

Tel 0141 287 2910
Fax 0141 226 8452
Email archives@gcl.glasgow.gov.uk
http://www.glasgow.gov.uk/gcl/
  home.htm

City Archivist: Mr AM Jackson
Open Mon–Th 9.30–4.45; Fri 9.30–4
Book in advance
Wheelchair access
Research service
P (Scotland)

**City of Glasgow, Mitchell Library
(code: 246)**
201 North Street, Glasgow G3 7DN

Tel 0141 287 2933
Fax 0141 287 2815
Email arts@gcl.glasgow.gov.uk

Departmental Librarian, Arts
  Department: Mr David Boyd
Open Mon–Thurs 9–8; Fri, Sat 9–5
Book in advance
Wheelchair access

**Highland Council Archive
(code: 232)**
Inverness Library, Farraline Park,
  Inverness IV1 1NH

Tel 01463 220330
Fax 01463 711128

Highland Council Archivist: Mr RD
  Steward
Open Mon–Thurs 10–1, 2–5
Book in advance
Wheelchair access

**North Highland Archive
(code: 1741)**
Wick Library, Sinclair Terrace, Wick
  KW1 5AB

Tel 01955 606432
Fax 01955 603000

Archivist: Brenda Lees
Open Mon, Tues, Thurs, Fri 10–1,
  2–5.30; Wed 10–1
Book in advance
No wheelchair access
Research service
P (Scotland)

**North Lanarkshire Archives
(code: 1778)**
10 Kelvin Road, Lenziemill,
  Cumbernauld G67 2BA

Tel 01236 737114
Fax 01236 781762

Archivist: Mr Craig Geddes
Open Mon–Fri 9–5
Book in advance
Wheelchair access

**South Lanarkshire Council
Archives and Information
Management Service (code: 1828)**
30 Hawbank Road, College Milton,
  East Kilbride G74 5EX

Tel 01355 239193
Fax 01355 242365

Archivist: Mr Frank Rankin
Open by appointment only
Proof of ID required
Book in advance
Wheelchair access
Research service

**West Lothian Council Archives
(code: 1829)**
7 Rutherford Square, Brucefield,
  Livingston, West Lothian EH54
  9BU

Tel 01506 460020
Fax 01506 416167
http://www.westlothian.gov.uk/
  libraries/

Archivist: Miss Alice Stewart
Open Mon–Thurs 9–5; Fri 9–4
Proof of ID required
Book in advance
Wheelchair access

**Midlothian Council Archives
(code: 584)**
Library Headquarters, 2 Clerk Street,
  Loanhead, Midlothian EH20 9DR

Tel 0131 271 3976
Fax 0131 440 4635
Email local.studies@
 midlothian.gov.uk
http://www.earl.org.uk/partners/
 midlothian/index.html

Archivist: Ms Ruth Calvert
Open Mon 9–5, 6–8; Tues–Thurs
 9–5; Fri 9–3.45
Proof of ID required
Wheelchair access

Orkney Archives (code: 241)
The Orkney Library, Laing Street,
 Kirkwall KW15 1NW

Tel 01856 873166/875260
Fax 01856 875260

Principal Archivist: Miss Alison
 Fraser
Open Mon–Fri 9–1, 2–4.45. Closed
 three weeks in mid-February
Book in advance
Wheelchair access
P (Scotland)

**Perth and Kinross Council Archive
(code: 252)**
AK Bell Library, 2–8 York Place, Perth
 PH2 8EP

Tel 01738 477012
Fax 01738 477010
Email library@pkc.gov.uk
http://www.pkc.gov.uk/

Archivist: Mr Stephen Connelly
Open Mon–Fri 9.30–5
Book in advance
Wheelchair access
Research service
P (Scotland)

**Scottish Borders Archive and Local
History Centre (code: 1097)**
Library Headquarters, St Mary's Mill,
 Selkirk TD7 5EW

Tel 01750 20842
Fax 01750 22875

Principal Librarian Adult Services:
 Miss R Brown
Open Mon–Thurs 9–1, 2–5; Fri 9–1,
 2–3.30
Book in advance
Wheelchair access

Shetland Archives (code: 242)
44 King Harald Street, Lerwick ZE1
 0EQ

Tel 01595 696247
Fax 01595 696533
Email shetland.archives
 @zetnet.co.uk

Archivist: Mr Brian Smith
Open Mon–Thurs 9–1, 2–5; Fri 9–1,
 2–4
Wheelchair access
P (Scotland)

**Stirling Council Archives Services
(code: 224)**
Unit 6, Burghmuir Industrial Estate,
 Stirling FK7 7PY

Tel 01786 450745
Email archives@stirling-
 council.demon.co.uk

Council Archivist: Dr John Brims
Open Wed–Fri 10–12.30, 1.30–4.30
Proof of ID required
Book in advance
Wheelchair access
Research service
P (Scotland)

Part 3: Other Repositories

NORTHERN IRELAND

Public Record Office of Northern Ireland (code: 255)
66 Balmoral Avenue, Belfast BT9 6NY

Tel 01232 255905
  (028 9025 5905)
Fax 01232 255999
  (028 9025 5999)
Email proni@nics.gov.uk
http://proni.nics.gov.uk/

Chief Executive: post vacant
Deputy Ch. Exec: Mr Gerry Slater
Open Mon–Wed, Fri 9.15–4.45;
  Thurs 9.15–8.45. Closed two weeks
  late November/early December
Readers ticket required (proof of ID
  in first instance)
Wheelchair access
P (Northern Ireland)

REPUBLIC OF IRELAND

Trinity College Library (code: 630)
College Street, Dublin 2, Ireland

Tel (00353 1) 677 2941
Fax (00353 1) 671 9003
http://www2.tcd.ie/
  Library/

Librarian: Mr Bill Simpson
Open Mon–Fri 10–5; Sat 10–1
Letter of introduction required
Book in advance
Special arrangements for wheelchairs

National Archives, Ireland (code: 625)
Bishop Street, Dublin 8, Ireland

Tel (00353 1) 407 2300
Fax (00353 1) 407 2333
Email mail@nationalarchives.ie
http://www.nationalarchives.ie

Director: Dr David Craig
Open Mon–Fri 10–5
Readers ticket required
Wheelchair access

National Library of Ireland (code: 624)
Kildare Street, Dublin 2, Ireland

Tel (00353 1) 661 8811
Fax (00353 1) 676 6690
http://www.hea.ie/natlib/

Keeper of Manuscripts: Dr Noel
  Kissane
Open Mon–Thurs 10–12.40, 2–5.15,
  6.15–9; Fri 10–12.40, 2–5.15;
  Sat 10–1
Readers ticket required (proof of ID
  in first instance)
Special arrangements for wheelchairs
Research service

Representative Church Body Library (code: 628)
Braemor Park, Churchtown, Dublin
  14, Ireland

Tel (00353 1) 492 3979
Fax (00353 1) 492 4770
Email library@ireland.anglican.org
http://www.ireland.anglican.org/
  library.html

Librarian and Archivist: Dr Raymond
  Refaussé
Open Mon–Fri 9.30–1, 1.45–5
Special arrangements for wheelchairs

GUERNSEY

**States of Guernsey Island Archives
Service (code: 828)**
29 Victoria Road, St Peter Port,
  Guernsey GY1 1HU

Tel 01481 724512
Fax 01481 715814

Island Archivist: Dr DM Ogier
Open Mon–Fri 8.30–12.30, 1.30–4.30
Book in advance
No wheelchair access
P (Guernsey)

JERSEY

**Jersey Archives Service
(code: 1539)**
The Weighbridge, St Helier, Jersey
  JE2 3NF

Tel 01534 633303
Fax 01534 633301
http://www.jersey.gov.uk/
  jerseyarchives/index.html

Head of Archives Service:
  Mrs Denise Williams
Open Mon–Fri 9–5
Proof of ID required
Book in advance
Special arrangements for wheelchairs
Research service
P (Jersey)

ISLE OF MAN

Isle of Man Public Record Office
Unit 3, Spring Valley Industrial
  Estate, Braddan, Douglas, Isle of
  Man IM2 2QR

Tel 01624 613383
Fax 01624 613384
Email public.records@registry.gov.im
http://www.gov.im/deptindex/
  reginfo.html

Public Records Officer: Miss Miriam
  Critchlow
Open Mon–Thus 8.30–5.30;
  Fri 8.30–5
Proof of ID required
Readers should contact the relevant
  department and make an
  appointment to see original material
No wheelchair access
P (Isle of Man)

**Manx National Heritage Library
(code: 147)**
Manx Museum and National Trust,
  Douglas, Isle of Man IM1 3LY

Tel 01624 648000
Fax 01624 648001
Email enquiries@m&h.gov.im

Librarian/Archivist: Mr Roger Sims
Open Mon–Sat 10–5
Proof of ID required (letter of
  introduction preferred for off-island
  visitors)
Book in advance
Wheelchair access
P (Isle of Man) D (Sodor and Man)

Part 4: Register Offices

Family Records Centre
1 Myddelton Street, London EC1R
   1UW

Tel 0181 392 5300 (general enquiries)
   (020 8392 5300)
0171 233 9233 (certificate enquiries)
   (020 7233 9233)
Fax 0181 392 5307
   (020 8392 5307)
Minicom 0181 392 5308
   (020 8392 5308)
Email certificate.services@
   ons.gov.uk (certificate enquiries)
http://www.pro.gov.uk/about/frc/

Public Record Office Manager:
   Mrs Margaret Brennand
Office for National Statistics
   Manager: Mrs Marily Troyano
Open Mon, Wed, Fri 9–5; Tues 10–7;
   Thurs 9–7; Sat 9.30–5. Closed Sat
   before bank holidays
Wheelchair access

Jointly run by the Public Record
Office and the Office for National
Statistics. Holds indexes of statutory
registers of births, marriages and
deaths in England and Wales since
1837 and microform copies of Census
of Population returns 1841–1891,
Estate Duty Office death duty
registers 1796–1858, copies of wills
and administrations before 1858 from
the Prerogative Court of Canterbury
and non-parochial registers

**Principal Registry of the Family
Division**
1st Avenue House, 42–49 High
   Holborn, London WC1V 6NP

Tel 0171 936 7000
   (020 7936 7000)

Senior District Judge:
   Mr GBNA Angel
Open Mon–Fri 10–4.30
P

Holds copies of all wills admitted to
probate in England and Wales and all
grants of probate and administration
issued since 1858

**General Register Office for
Scotland**
New Register House, Edinburgh EH1
   3YT

Tel 0131 334 0380
Fax 0131 314 4400
Email nrh.gros@gtnet.gov.uk
http://www.open.gov.uk/gros/
   groshome.htm

Registrar General for Scotland:
   Mr John Randall
Open Mon–Fri 9–4.30

Has custody of all statutory registers
of births, marriages and deaths in
Scotland since 1855, Scottish parish
registers 1553–1854 and census
records 1841–91

**General Register Office
(Northern Ireland)**
Oxford House, 49–55 Chichester
  Street, Belfast BT1 4HL

Tel 01232 252000
  (028 9025 2000)
Fax 01232 252044
  (028 9025 2044)
http://www.nics.gov.uk/nisra/gro/

Registrar General: Dr Norman Caven
Open Mon–Fri 9.30–4

Has custody of all statutory registers
of marriages in Northern Ireland
since 1845 and births and deaths
since 1864

Greffe (code: 745)
Royal Court House, St Peter Port,
  Guernsey GY1 2PB

Tel 01481 725277
Fax 01481 715097
Email HM_Greffier@court1.
  guernsey.gov.uk

HM Greffier: Mr KH Tough
Open Mon–Fri 9–1, 2–4
Letter of introduction required
Book in advance
Wheelchair access

Judicial Greffe (code 1939)
Morier House, Halkett Place, St
  Helier, Jersey JE1 1DD

Tel 01534 502300
Fax 01534 502399
Email jgreffe@super.net.uk
http://www.jersey.gov.uk/

Judicial Greffier: Mr M Wilkins
Registrar: Mrs J Hume
Open Mon–Fri 9–1, 2–5.15
Book in advance

Has custody of the records of the
Royal Court, Public Registry of
Deeds and Probate Registry.

Civil Registry (Isle of Man)
Registries Building, Bucks Road,
  Douglas, Isle of Man IM1 3AR

Tel 01624 687039
Fax 01624 685296
http://www.gov.im/

Civil Registrar: Mrs SK Cain
Open Mon–Fri 9–1, 2–5

Has custody of all statutory registers
of births and deaths in the Isle of
Man since 1878, marriages since 1883
and records of Church of England
baptisms, marriages and burials
earlier than these dates

Part 5: Related Organisations

British Records Association
c/o London Metropolitan Archives,
   40 Northampton Road, London
   EC1R 0HB

Tel 0171 833 0428
   (020 7833 0428)
Fax 0171 833 0416
   (020 7833 0416)

Archivist: Ms SK Henning

Exists to promote and encourage
the work of all individuals and
institutions interested in the
conservation and use of records.
Its Records Preservation Section
arranges the deposit in appropriate
repositories of documents received
mainly from the offices of London
solicitors

Business Archives Council
3rd & 4th Floors, 101 Whitechapel
   High Street, London E1 7RE

Tel 0171 247 0024
   (020 7247 0024)
Fax 0171 422 0026
   (020 7422 0026)
Email bac@archives.gla.ac.uk
http://www.archives.gla.ac.uk/bac/

Manager:
   Ms Sharon Quinn-Robinson

Promotes the efficient management,
preservation and use of business
records through publications,
training and practical support

**Business Archives Council of
Scotland**
c/o Glasgow University Archives and
   Business Record Centre, 77–87
   Dumbarton Road, Glasgow G11
   6PW

Tel 0141 330 4159
Fax 0141 330 4158
Email bacs@archives.gla.ac.uk
http://www.archives.gla.ac.uk/bacs/

Surveying Officer: Ms Johanna King

Performs similar functions to the
Business Archives Council and also
provides advice regarding business
records which are under threat of
dispersal or destruction

**Institute of Heraldic and
Genealogical Studies**
Northgate, Canterbury CT1 1BA

Tel 01227 768664
Fax 01227 765617
Email ihgs@ihgs.ac.uk
http://www.ihgs.ac.uk/

Principal: Mr Cecil Humphery-Smith

A school for the study of the history
and structure of the family and of
subjects generally auxiliary to
historical applications

London University, Institute of Historical Research

School of Advanced Study, University of London, Senate House, Malet Street, London WC1E 7HU

Tel 0171 862 8740
(020 7862 8740)
Fax 0171 436 2183
(020 7436 2183)
Email ihr@sas.ac.uk
http://ihr.sas.ac.uk/

Director: Professor David Cannadine
Open Mon–Fri 9–8.45; Sat 9–4.45
Letter of introduction required
A fee may be payable
Wheelchair access

Acts a nexus for historical researchers throughout the world. Has an open-access library, publishes works of reference, administers research projects, runs conferences and administers awards. Maintains *History*, the Internet gateway for resources for historians

Royal Commission on Historical Manuscripts

Quality House, Quality Court, Chancery Lane, London WC2A 1HP

Tel 0171 242 1198
(020 7242 1198)
Fax 0171 831 3550
(020 7831 3550)
Email nra@hmc.gov.uk
http://www.hmc.gov.uk/

Secretary: Dr CJ Kitching
Open Mon–Fri 9.30–5
No wheelchair access

Acts as a central clearing-house for information about the nature and location of historical manuscripts and papers outside the Public Records. The National Register of Archives and the Manorial Documents Register are available for public use in its search room and via the Internet. Also maintains ARCHON, the archival gateway for Internet resources for British archivists and researchers

Scottish Records Association

c/o Glasgow City Archives, Mitchell Library, 201 North Street, Glasgow G3 7DN

Tel 0141 287 2914
Fax 0141 226 8452
Email archives@gcl.glasgow.gov.uk

Chairman: Dr Athol Murray
Treasurer: Mr Robert Urquhart

Society of Archivists

40 Northampton Road, London EC1R 0HB

Tel 0171 278 8630
(020 7278 8630)
Fax 0171 278 2107
(020 7278 2107)
Email societyofarchivists@ archives.org.uk
http://www.archives.org.uk/

Chairman: Mr Patrick Cadell
Executive Secretary: Mr Patrick Cleary

The recognised professional body of archivists, records managers and archive conservators in the United Kingdom and the Republic of Ireland

Society of Genealogists
14 Charterhouse Buildings, Goswell
  Road, London EC1M 7BA

Tel 0171 251 8799
  (020 7251 8799)
Fax 0171 250 1800
  (020 7250 1800)
Email library@sog.org.uk
http://www.sog.org.uk/

Director and Secretary: Mr Robert
  Gordon
Open Tues, Fri, Sat 10–6; Wed, Thurs
  10–8. Closed first week in February

Its genealogical reference library is
open to non members on payment of
a fee. Holds lists of the names and
addresses of regional genealogical
societies and of individual
professional research workers in this
field, as well as working papers of
genealogical researchers

Index